Penguin Critical Studies

Sense and Sensibility

Isobel Armstrong has been Professor of English at Birkbeck College, University of London, since 1989. She held the Chair of English at the University of Southampton before that. She was educated at the Friends' School, Saffron Walden, and graduated from Leicester University. She has taught at the universities of Leicester and Princeton and is the author of *Victorian Scrutinies*, Victorian reviews of poetry, and *Language as Living Form in 19th Century Poetry*, a study of Romantic and Victorian poetic language in the light of Hegelian philosophy. She has also published a critical study of *Mansfield Park* for this series and *Victorian Poetry: Poetry, Politics and Poetics* (1993). In addition to editing a volume of nineteenth-century women poets, she is embarking on a study of glass in Victorian culture.

025660

Penguin Critical Studies
Series Editor: Brian Loughrey

Jane Austen

Sense and Sensibility

Isobel Armstrong

Penguin Books

PENGUIN BOOKS

Published by the Penguin Group
Penguin Books Ltd, 27 Wrights Lane, London W8 5TZ, England
Penguin Books USA Inc., 375 Hudson Street, New York, New York 10014, USA
Penguin Books Australia Ltd, Ringwood, Victoria, Australia
Penguin Books Canada Ltd, 10 Alcorn Avenue, Toronto, Ontario, Canada M4V 3B2
Penguin Books (NZ) Ltd, 182–190 Wairau Road, Auckland 10, New Zealand

Penguin Books Ltd, Registered Offices: Harmondsworth, Middlesex, England

First published 1994

10 9 8 7 6 5 4 3 2

Filmset by Datix International Limited, Bungay, Suffolk
Printed in England by Clays Ltd, St Ives plc
Set in 9/11 pt Monophoto Times

To Helen Carr, Laura Marcus and Carol Watts, with thanks for their help

Contents

Introduction

The title

Sense and Sensibility: Jane Austen could hardly have chosen two words more weighted with accumulated cultural meaning for the title of her first published novel in 1811. These abstract nouns throw out a challenge – political, aesthetic, religious and philosophical – to the eighteenth century and to her own contemporary world; and the more so as, by 1811, the semantic range of 'sense' and 'sensibility' was shifting and contested ground. It is not even clear whether the title expresses an antithesis between the two terms as mutually exclusive qualities, sense or sensibility, or whether the conjunction, 'and', represents conjoined, overlapping attributes, which mutually reinforce one another, sense *and* sensibility.

The most obvious signification of the title, a psychological one, designating the mental characteristics of individuals in the novel, and seemingly pointing to the subjectivity of the two girls who are its heroines, does not seem to be fully adequate to the experiences portrayed in the text. For one thing, the nouns of the title are used very infrequently, and scarcely at all with reference to the two main characters, Elinor and Marianne. But neither do they encompass the extremes of the novel. When the crisis of Willoughby's rejection of Marianne finally breaks, Elinor 'felt immediately such a sickness at heart as made her hardly able to hold up her head' (Chapter 29, p. 153), and gives way 'to a burst of tears, which at first was scarcely less violent than Marianne's', while Marianne, 'covering her face with her handkerchief, almost *screamed* with agony' (p. 154, emphasis added). The grief is too intense – verging on hysteria – to warrant the description 'sensibility'. The narrative seems to miss the calibrations of its title. Among the male characters it concerns itself with the low-grade melancholia such as Edward Ferrars experiences, with the concealed anxiety state of Colonel Brandon, right through to Willoughby's reckless pleasure-seeking and Sir John Middleton's compulsive – and coercive – pursuit of group enjoyments. Some of these men exemplify desperate forms of male hysteria as violent as anything Marianne displays. If we are to seek for what characterizes this work, it is a certain sadness and tension and even at times an almost lyrical sombreness.

1

Samuel Johnson's *Dictionary of the English Language* (1755) helps one to gain some understanding of the possible range of signification of 'sense' and 'sensibility' in the eighteenth century.[1] Jane Austen was born twenty years after the dictionary was published, and though the terms accrued meanings Johnson does not always mention, his attempt to define and fix usage provides a starting point.

Johnson lists ten meanings for the word 'sense'. The first is a physiological property: 'faculty or power by which external objects are perceived; the sight; touch; hearing; smell; taste'. Second is what these senses enable one to experience: 'perception by the senses; sensation'. Third is a mental attribute: 'perception of intellect; apprehension of mind'. Johnson allies this ability to grasp things with 'quick', meaning not only rapid, but also vital, alive. Fourthly, sense is defined as 'sensibility; quickness or keenness of perception'. Fifth is a faculty we would probably put as the primary meaning of 'sense' today, 'understanding; soundness of faculties; strength of natural reason'. The sixth meaning is 'reason; reasonable meaning' – Johnson here means that which makes coherent sense. Seventh is 'opinion; notion; judgement'. Eight is 'consciousness; conviction'. Ninth is 'moral perception'. Lastly, tenth is 'meaning, import', that is, signification.

What is striking is that 'sense' is much nearer to the meanings, 'sense data' and the 'faculties for perceiving sense data' than modern meanings of the word are. 'Sense' moves through physiological experience to the soundness of perception, which presupposes reliable truth claims and from there to ethical perception. What is missing is a context for thinking of 'sense' in terms of practical common sense or limiting rationality. It is an attribute we might associate with 'sense' today but it is simply not there in Johnson's *Dictionary*. More surprising still, 'sensibility' is a sub-category or an attribute of 'sense'. Johnson lists 'sensibility' as a word in its own right, of course, but he does not refer to the intensification of meaning which the word received as a result of becoming both a literary and an experiential or cultural category, a recognized form or style of responding to the world. One could speak of the novel of sensibility, for instance, and, by extension, of sensibility virtually as a mode of living and of experiencing phenomena, but Johnson excludes such notions. The great cult of sensibility prevalent in the eighteenth century, the deliberate practice of seeing ethical, social and psychological experience through an overdetermined emphasis (an emphasis in excess of what seems necessary) on feeling and emotion as cause and effect of value, is absent. Whether this occurs as a result of his own firm and possibly unconscious repressions, or because the 'cult' of sensibility was not so culturally noticeable as it was to be later in the century, or because his understanding of dictionary-making excluded this kind of reference, it is not easy to see.[2]

'Sensibility' is given three meanings: first, 'sensibleness; perception'. Johnson means, so far as one can see from the context of his illustrative quotations, awareness, almost alertness. Secondly, sensibility means 'quickness of sensation', and thirdly, 'quickness of perception; delicacy'. What Johnson expresses is the speed, rapidity and *vitality* associated with sensibility, as well as its close union with bodily experience. For sensibility is a faculty of mind and the senses. It is almost as if, for him, sensibility is sense intensified and refined. 'Delicacy' is an element which, in Johnson's taxonomy, is not associated with sense, but only with sensibility. 'Delicacy' became increasingly gendered and feminized as the century progressed. In 1792 in her *Vindication of the Rights of Woman* delicacy was the female characteristic castigated by Mary Wollstonecraft, and for her it was a purely physical rather than a mental attribute. It meant the assumption of artificial weakness and led to actual weakness as women starved and mutilated their bodies in the service of 'exquisite sensibility'.[3] In her reading, sensibility has negated its connection with vitality and energy.

Perhaps the cognate word, 'sensible', for which Johnson adduces eight meanings, suggests how closely related sense and sensibility could be. It is convenient to list these meanings as a frame of reference for the two words. One: 'having the power of perceiving by the senses'. Two: 'perception by the senses'. Three: 'perceived by the mind'. Four: 'perceiving by either mind or senses'. Five: 'having a moral perception; having the quality of being affected by moral good or ill'. Six: 'having quick intellectual feeling; being easily or strongly affected'. Seven: 'convinced, persuaded' (a colloquial use, Johnson adds). Eight: 'in conversation it has sometimes the sense of reasonable; judicious; wise'. Interestingly, moral and aesthetic signification is entwined here, just as mental and physical experience is called up in the semantic range Johnson attributes to 'sensible'.

Johnson's *Dictionary* allows us to make some preliminary assumptions about the mid-eighteenth-century meanings of 'sense' and 'sensibility'. In the first place, the two qualities are in many ways allied. They share an emphasis on the senses and on alertness of perception, vitality and energy. But though the word 'sensible' combines the moral and aesthetic, the body and the mind, its properties bifurcate in 'sense' and 'sensibility'. Coherence, meaning, judgement, ethics, and an emphasis on the hermeneutic, interpretative aspects of reflection and perception are included in the attributes of 'sense'. On the other hand, sense perception and the aesthetic quality of delicacy or fineness of awareness, and the achievement of *insight* through these aesthetic qualities rather than *understanding* through recourse to meaning and intellect, appear to separate out sensibility from sense. Though Johnson's readings of both words are not stable, and certainly overlap, it is possible to arrive at different emphases.

But both 'sense' and 'sensibility' are truly 'complex words', as William Empson would have termed them, and require delicate semantic reconstruction.[4] And this is before any attempt has been made to consider the archaeology of 'sense' and 'sensibility' as they were understood in terms of literary and philosophical movements, and their specialized vocabularies, in late eighteenth-century culture. Given this difficulty, though it certainly helps to consider the abstract significance of the words of Jane Austen's title, the strategy of this discussion will be to approach the categories of 'sense' and 'sensibility' obliquely, allowing the words of the title to gain meanings through an exploration of the particularities of the text, through other key words and topoi, and through form, the configuration and grouping of characters and the way the narrative is ordered.

It is possible that Jane Austen was so economical with the terms of her title in the novel itself because she wishes her readers to rediscover and redefine its meaning through the action of the text. Therefore I will postpone further discussion of the meaning of the words 'sense' and 'sensibility' until they have achieved a richer content, and until their full implications emerge, in the course of an exploration of the novel.

The novel's position within Jane Austen's other works

Though *Sense and Sensibility* was Jane Austen's first published novel, it was by no means the first she had written. It was the product of a long and vigorously pursued engagement with writing. *Sense and Sensibility*, first drafted as an epistolary novel over 1795–6 as *Elinor and Marianne*, was twice revised before publication, in 1797 and 1809. Meanwhile she had attempted to publish *Lady Susan*, probably written over 1793–4, and *First Impressions*, completed in 1797 and subsequently revised as *Pride and Prejudice*. *Northanger Abbey* was also written over 1798–9, and it would be right to say that before *Sense and Sensibility* was revised for the last time, Jane Austen had already completed the work of her early years, and this, perhaps strangely, makes *Sense and Sensibility* almost a mature work, almost a part of the oeuvre belonging to her later period of writing, relating as much to *Mansfield Park* (1814) as to

Pride and Prejudice; perhaps this explains its sombre quality. Nevertheless, the novel is also a summa of earlier themes, and one can turn to the extravaganza, *Love and Freindship*, written when Jane Austen was fourteen, to see this.

Love and Freindship provides a useful preface to *Sense and Sensibility* because it makes prolific use of the overt vocabulary of sensibility with which the later novel is so sparing and because it treats with almost brazen directness the concerns which become a cautious subtext in *Sense and Sensibility*. Rightly described as 'exuberant' by one of its recent critics, this epistolary novel is written with the high nervous tension, comic intensity and surreal insouciance which is generally associated with Sterne's *Tristram Shandy* rather than with Jane Austen's work.[5] At the start of the novel a knock on the door is an occasion for elaborate verbal exchange on the part of a family, until the maid enters with 'the most beauteous and amiable Youth I had ever beheld. The servant, she kept to herself' (Letter 5). The vocabulary of sensibility is repeatedly used with the same satirical energy and parodic flourish. 'A sensibility too tremblingly alive to every affliction of my Freinds, my Acquaintance and particularly to every affliction of my own, was my only fault, if a fault it could be called' (Letter 3). Augusta, sister of the 'husband' of Laura, the narrator, had 'none of that interesting Sensibility or amiable Simpathy in her manners' (Letter 7), while another first acquaintance, Sophia, 'was all Sensibility and Feeling. We flew into each other's arms and after having exchanged vows of mutual Friendship for the rest of our Lives, instantly unfolded to each other the most inward Secrets of our Hearts' (Letter 8).

This early piece grasps the external features of the literature of sensibility, the disqualification from sentiment earned by a failure to read Goethe's *Sorrows of Werter* (Letter 12), for instance, or the capacity for physical weakness in a heroine expressed in the notorious 'We fainted alternately on a Sofa' (Letter 8). It satirizes the dominant trope of retirement – 'I who am doomed to waste my Days of Youth and Beauty in an humble Cottage in the vale of Usk' (Letter 4) – and mimics the affective vocabularies of pastoral and madness in the novel of feeling. But its critique goes much further than external features of style. It sees the voraciousness which belongs dialectically to narcissistic sentiment. Sophia's husband is imprisoned in Newgate ('a Blow to our Gentle Sensibility'), but she will not see him, arguing that it is enough to *feel* pity by simply hearing of his distress and that to see him would only distress her. '"I cannot go to Newgate; I shall not be able to support the sight of my Augustus in so cruel a confinement – my feelings are sufficiently shocked by the *recital*, of his Distress, but to behold it will overpower my Sensibility"' (Letter 10). So much for fake empathy: the text grasps that *feeling* has become a substitute for ethics, for analysis and action, and even for interpersonal relationships. In the same way, at about the same time, in *Songs of Experience* (1794), Blake saw that pity was a substitute for real social action: 'Pity would be no more, / If we did not make somebody Poor' ('The Human Abstract').

Love and Freindship also remorselessly satirizes the centrality of the 'natural' ties of family to the literature of sensibility by showing how shallow family bonds are. Laura and her associates disobey and steal from their families without compunction: Augustus had 'gracefully purloined' a considerable sum of money 'from his Unworthy father's Escritoire' (Letter 9), before marrying Sophia. Relationship is invariably connected with finance and is the occasion for extortion: when a tortuous illegitimate relationship with a titled grandfather through an 'Italian opera girl' is disclosed; 'we agreed to endeavour to *get something from him* by discovering the relationship' (Letter 15, emphasis added). The emphasis on money deconstructs the notion that the small family unit, bonded through affective ties, is the paradigm of ethical and social relationships. Moreoever, the mystical aura of family, in which affinity and filiation are instantly recognized by the members of the group (even when strangers to one another) through inborn sympathy and intuition, is burlesqued with intense irony. Laura discovers her grand-father on one of her picaresque journeys: 'At his first Appearance my Sensibility was wonderfully affected and e'er I gazed at him a 2d time, an instinctive Sympathy whispered to my Heart, that he was my Grandfather' (Letter 11). She throws herself on her knees before him and he responds with reciprocal recognition.

He started, and having attentively examined my features, raised me from the Ground and throwing his Grandfatherly arms around my neck, exclaimed, 'Acknowledge thee Yes dear resemblance of my Laurina and my Laurina's Daughter, sweet image of my Claudia and my Claudia's mother.' (Letter 11)

But the bliss does not last. After discovering four grandchildren in quick succession ('I am the son of Agatha, your Laurina's 4th and Youngest daughter'), he departs hastily after distributing small sums of money. Family bonds do not hold.

Jane Austen's *Love and Freindship* has the energy – and the meanness – of early picaresque writing such as that by Fielding and Smollett. It may not bear an immediate resemblance to *Sense and Sensibility*, where Elinor and Marianne and their family, in their enforced retirement to their cottage near Exeter, actually belong to a series of other people's picaresque novels, staying still while their visitors enter and depart, but both novels make an enquiry into the nature of family, its meaning and its obligations. *Love and Freindship* uses two words insistently repeated in *Sense and Sensibility*, 'attachment', meaning both a love relationship and a legal relationship, engagement, or marriage, and 'connection', meaning both a social association and a family bond. It satirizes the logic of love at first sight, which must mean that 'The Attachment must be reciprocal': after a character has 'pleaded his Attachment', he automatically elopes to Gretna Green (Letter 12). It also burlesques the opposing meanings of 'connection', which imply both choice and determinism. Augusta reproaches her brother with an 'imprudent connection' with Laura (Letter 7), an act of choice, but at the end of the novel, Laura conveniently, as if through the inevitability of fate, rediscovers her family: 'Is it possible that I should so unexpectedly be surrounded by my nearest Relations and Connections?' (Letter 14). In *Sense and Sensibility* these words are progressively deepened and made more complex. Though the meanings of 'sense' and 'sensibility' and the distribution of attributes they imply are open to definition, they can be partly stabilized by relating 'sense' to Elinor's scrupulous, sensitive rationality and 'sensibility' to the volatile Marianne. The unobtrusive words 'attachment' and 'connection' prove to be even more open to definition than the nouns of the title. Yet they go to the heart of the narrative. They give a deeper social and psychological content to the words 'sense' and 'sensibility'. And they indicate, as scarcely noticeable words so often do in Jane Austen's texts, that one is reading a much more impassioned novel than one had first thought.

Section One
Family: Making the Right Connections

Sense and Sensibility is shadowed by three dead or absent fathers or figures of authority: Jane Austen's own father, the reigning King, George III (1760–1820), and Hamlet's father, King Hamlet. The novel begins with a double death, the death of Mr Dashwood senior, owner of Norland, and, a year after, the death of Henry Dashwood, his nephew and the father of the three girls, Elinor, Marianne and Margaret. To expose and explore strains within the social fabric and the family – not simply an emblem of the nation but an extension of it – Jane Austen subtracts the father figure from her novel. The male of the older generation, his power and patriarchal authority, is absent from the text.

At the beginning of the novel the three girls and their mother are in mourning, double-mourning, and they suffer a third trauma when they are ousted from their home and move to a cottage in the West Country. When Marianne wanders in the grounds of Norland on the eve of their departure, uttering the apostrophes of the literary conventions of elegy, it is worth remembering that she is in mourning, however banal her words: 'Dear, dear Norland . . . when shall I cease to regret you! – when learn to feel at home elsewhere! Oh! happy house, could you know what I suffer in now viewing you from this spot, from whence perhaps I may view you no more!' (Chapter 5, p. 23) Banality is after all the mourner's fate. We are told how Marianne and Mrs Dashwood work upon one another's grief: 'The agony of grief which overpowered them at first, was voluntarily renewed, was sought for, was created again and again' (Chapter 1, p. 6). Elinor's alarm and her attempt to repress this grief solicits the reader to a similarly embarrassed repression of feeling. But though so much of the novel is told from Elinor's point of view, the text often evades her control with consummate skill. This grief is embarrassing, is excessive, but it is there. It may be preferable to the subdued depression which dogs Elinor for so much of the novel. It is easy to miss the emphasis on 'created' in this account of sorrow. Even at this date the word suggested a positive act of making.

The death of the father means a world of older women and widows, husbandless women as well as fatherless daughters. Widows or women without husbands become the heads of families. Mrs Dashwood is joined by the insensitive joker and matchmaker, Mrs Jennings, mother of Lady Middleton, wife of the Dashwoods' new landlord and patron, and mother also of Charlotte, married to the young Mr Palmer. The pattern of widow and two fatherless girls is repeated here. Widows also control sons and son figures. Mrs Ferrars wields despotic power over Edward, her son, brother of the woman who evicts the Dashwoods from Norland. Edward's depressive condition – I have called it low-grade melancholia – deprived of control over his life and career – is apparent to Elinor when he arrives at the cottage to visit them. 'I think that I may defy many months to produce any good to me', Edward answers Elinor when she affirms that his mother must provide him with an 'independence': 'it must ere long become her happiness to prevent your whole youth from being wasted in discontent' (Chapter 19, p. 90). 'Wasted': this is strong language, suggesting as it does a lessening physical and sexual potency. But it is not only Edward for whom financial dependence has created an arrested oedipal block. Mrs Smith, the elderly relation on whom Willoughby is dependent for inheritance, is structurally in the same place as Mrs Ferrars with regard to Willoughby and wields almost as much power. She can send him away from her house when she knows of his seduction of a young girl, and she can summon him annually to stay with her. The only powerless older woman, in fact, is Mrs Dashwood herself.

Fatherless girls are doubled, or rather trebled, when the Steele sisters come on to the scene. They are orphans, wards of their uncle, and parallel the situation of Elinor and Marianne and Lady Middleton and Charlotte. But it testifies to Jane Austen's extraordinary fertility of invention that these multiple parallels and correspondences in familial patterns are never exactly the same. The Steele sisters are without a mother as well as a father: it is psychologically predictable that they will steal – the pun is presumably intended – love and affection, and compensate for their deprivation with money. But these incomplete families of girls and older women, though multiplied, are not so overdetermined as fatherless sons. Mr Palmer, Edward Ferrars, Robert Ferrars, whom Lucy Steele traps as a husband, Willoughby, John Dashwood, the half-brother of the three Dashwood girls, who inherits Norland and who lived apart from his father when his father took a second wife, and Sir John Middleton, the eternal child, all six share fatherlessness, even if in Sir John's case this is a metaphorical state. But Sir John's example only serves to show how the male figures appear not to be able to grow up.

What, then, is the significance of the three absent fathers, which

9

haunt this text: the Revd. George Austen, King George III and King Hamlet?

When Jane Austen began *Elinor and Marianne* her father was alive. By the time of the last revision, nearly fifteen years later, he was dead. Jane Austen had been living without him for four years when she revised *Sense and Sensibility* yet again in 1809. There had been three moves in the space of less than ten years after the long, settled period at Steventon: in 1801 to Bath, in 1806 to Southampton, and in 1809 to the house in Chawton – sometimes called a cottage – which her brother Edward found for his mother and sister. The death of Jane Austen's father must have marked a period of much greater vulnerability and insecurity for her. At the same time this death is associated with the upheaval of moves and changes of residence, with something very like homelessness. There seems to have been a significant pause in her literary activity round about this time, with an acceleration once she became settled at Chawton. The account of the move to Devon with only three servants, absolutely the minimum number of attendants required for the establishment of a gentleman, so nineteenth-century etiquette books inform us, suggests a familiarity with straitened means. The narrow stairs, the passage, not a hallway, which cuts through the house, the smoking kitchen, the two sixteen-foot square rooms (about the same size as those of a semi-detached house of the thirties), the by implication even smaller four bedrooms above them, the low-pitched room and the crooked ceiling noticed and rudely marked by Mr Palmer (Chapter 19), all these suggest the uneasy gentility to which the Dash-woods are reduced. The descriptions have the ring of experience.[6]

Jane Austen knew what it was like to be poor. This and the death of her father perhaps account for the sense of loss and the emotional intensity which wells up in the book; 'agony' is not a word usually associated with her prose. As important as this, however, is the uncanny experience of living in a patriarchal world in which the immediate heirs to and representatives of patriarchy are absent. Structures of power without their living embodiments? What kinds of constraint or licence does this produce? Jane Austen's loss, the subtraction of the father, must have prompted her to write a fiction which is a controlled experiment with a society without a vital constituent element, a symbolic order lacking in the obvious symbols of the law. What happens when this occurs? The husbandless and fatherless figures in this text seem to be acting, as will be seen, in a world where customary hierarchies are breaking down, or where they are being sustained for no meaningful reason. *Sense and Sensibility* is a mirror image of the later *Mansfield Park*, where the return of the father is the organizing principle of the novel.

The Revd. George Austen, King George III: this convergence of names is fortuitous but nevertheless significant. For George III, head of state and the symbolic father of the nation, was fatally flawed as a sustaining, sovereign figure of authority. He went mad over the years 1788–9, and though he recovered substantially, his mental condition was unstable, and its decline culminated in the Act of 1811, in which the Prince Regent took over full sovereign powers while remaining the King's substitute, a situation which had been anticipated by Pitt on the first occasion of the King's madness. Thus, throughout the period in which *Sense and Sensibility* was being drafted and redrafted (1795, 1797, 1809), the King's constitutional powers were weakening in both senses of the word, and the possibility of an heir substituting for but not *succeeding* to the absent father was a continual one.[7] The Prince was known to be a profligate libertine. It is interesting that there *are* legitimate heirs in the novel, but they are small boys who have nowhere near reached their majority, the rather nasty little sons of John Dashwood and Sir John Middleton respectively. Both kingship and heirship were problematical for the nation over a period of more than twenty years.

Perhaps the egocentric hedonism and rake's psychology, which are so clearly manifested by Willoughby, could be seen as a reflection of an incipient Regency culture, a longstanding literary convention of the rake adapted to a new political situation and betokening more than sexual danger. But almost more important is the will to compulsory social enjoyment on the part of so many characters, of which Sir John is the foremost. His addictive need to organize parties, and his almost panic-stricken desire to sit down with more than eight at table, is a source of comedy: 'they were all in high spirits and good humour, eager to be happy, and determined to submit to the greatest inconveniences and hardships rather than be otherwise' (Chapter 13, p. 56). But this has its dark side: the social engagements and the compulsively hectic enjoyments seem to be a defence against solitude; their displaced energies disavow and mask a blankness, a dread of emptiness. Sir John will do anything rather than confront an interiority which may not exist, and, perhaps, a marriage whose coldness is the other side of his empty warmth. The failure to grow up, characteristic of so many of the male figures, is another indicator that pre-Regency values have penetrated the text at a deep level of anxiety. Yet these values have also been subjected to analysis and critique through the patterns of the narrative itself, as it explores analogies between parallel characters and plays with different forms of immaturity. This immaturity is strangely coercive and exhausting. Marianne comments bitterly that 'The rent of this cottage is said to be low; but we have it on very hard terms', if the price of financial remission is the perpetual obligation to be unpaid companions to the Middleton family.

Compulsive and compulsory cheerfulness is not only a way of blocking melancholia; it is also a refusal to recognize the pressure of disturbing events. King George III was a beleaguered king, quite apart from his mental instability. There was a war on against France, first against revolutionary and subsequently against Napoleonic France, from 1793 to 1815 with a brief respite in 1801. A war economy and ideological conflict at home, and a draining war abroad, were the conditions under which *Sense and Sensibility* was written. The upturn of the war did not occur until after the novel was published.

In her juvenile *The History of England*, Jane Austen attacks the 'Gang' run by Cromwell, which was responsible for the death of Charles I and who 'may be considered as the original Causers of all the disturbances Distresses and Civil Wars in which England for many years was embroiled'. Charles, she says, can be vindicated from the charge of 'Arbitrary and tyrannical government'. The threat of the French revolution meant that republican ideas were once again in circulation in the late eighteenth century. Marilyn Butler has described this time of radical ferment, when such bodies as the Revolution Society, the Society of Friends of the People, and the Corresponding Society, flourished – all of which were promulgating revolutionary theories – as a war of ideas.[8] The initial public approval of the French revolution in England had suffered a backlash well before England went to war with France in 1793. There were riots in Birmingham in support of the King in 1791, for instance. Anti-Jacobinism was encouraged by repression from above: between 1792 and 1800 Pitt oversaw a series of repressive measures; the persecution of reformers began in 1792 with a Royal Proclamation against 'seditious writings', which continued in 1793–4 with the treason trials and the suspension of Habeas Corpus, and in 1795 with the Two Acts which forbade the speaking or writing of treason as well as acts of treason. Stamp duties were imposed on newspapers and the registration of printing presses was required in 1796. Legislation banning workers' combinations was put in place over 1799–1800.[9]

Fear of the overthrow of authority and control, with a proportionate fear of authority's excess, work in contrary motion in *Sense and Sensibility*, creating that sense of blockage and stalemate which often slows the novel, and suggesting energies thwarted or sapped. Marianne, with her volatile emotions and reckless 'revolutionary' temperament, loving the freedom of outside spaces, impatient of restraint and willing to give the feelings uncontrolled expression, is often seen as the paradigmatic Jacobin. If she is such a figure, however, she must be seen in relation to the anxious need for control and discipline which Elinor suffers in excess, prematurely repressing the act of mourning both in the crises of their father's death and Willoughby's rejection. What should be a dialectic between Elinor and Marianne, in which conflict could be resolved, often turns into a stationary, obstructive contradiction, whose end can only be illness, as is finally Marianne's lot.[10] Unable to accept Elinor's loving surveillance and her model of self-control in the extremity of her grief over Willoughby, Marianne falls ill. The novel is marked by a double movement of long, slow waiting and hectic, almost manic, activity. Willoughby's dramatic rush to the sick Marianne and the waiting Elinor is an episode typical of the rhythm of the narration.

In contrast to such moments of violence is the debilitating check on energies, from Edward's lassitude to Lady Middleton's insipidity. Throughout the novel Elinor is forced into inaction. She can only wait – and control herself. When Lucy Steele tells her the news of her longstanding engagement with Edward, 'she could hardly stand' (Chapter 22, p. 114), but endeavours to achieve 'a composure of voice' (Chapter 22, p. 114). Nothing that happens in the novel, good or bad, comes about as the result of her actions. The long, patient but sapping wait is the fate of many in the novel; Edward, Elinor, Colonel Brandon, even the unsympathetic Steeles, are forced into this impotence. It is as if the war mentality, the prolonged inaction associated with civilian experience of a long and interminable war, has imposed itself on the experience of these characters and on the mood of the book. Until 1807, when success in the Peninsular War began, Napoleon's power seemed invincible. Despite successful naval battles such as the Battle of the Nile (1798), France won an inexorable series of victories: and by 1806, Britain was isolated; Pitt and Nelson were dead. High inflation between 1793 and 1801, associated both with bad harvests and the trading embargo of the Orders in Council, produced urban and agrarian poverty. The speculative boom connected with the war economy collapsed in 1811.[11] Two of Jane Austen's brothers were in the navy. These events are apparent, not in the content of the novel but in the psychic experience it portrays and in the rhythms of the narrative.

In the equations of war, which so unobtrusively shape the novel, Colonel Brandon's presence cannot be ignored. He is a rich man, enviably rich to Willougby, who, in one of the fantasies of orientalism rare in Jane Austen's work, imputes to Brandon access to 'nabobs, gold mohrs, and palanquins' (Chapter 10, p. 45); his snobbery and dislike were common attitudes. It is not clear whether Brandon is one of the East India officers who made huge fortunes in India, trading independently, bargaining with local rulers and exploiting resources. At any rate, Brandon is an outsider, one of the returned Anglo Indians, who were regarded with a mixture of envy, suspicion and contempt as 'Plunderers of the East'. It was often said that Pitt paid for the French wars with colonial gold and silver invested in British banks.[12] In Brandon the vilified colonial outsider moves to the centre, a process about which the text is uneasy and ambivalent. He is a man of honour, but he has a shadowy colonial past. He wins Marianne, but how legitimate are his riches and how secure his public standing? Jane Austen's brothers were involved with the East India Company. The worry is near to home.

The year after *Sense and Sensibility* was published, in 1812, the radical Mrs Barbauld published a poem, *Eighteen Hundred and Eleven*. This poem, possibly inspired by the Regency Act, condemned the war with France and portrayed a decadent Britain on the verge of collapse, her trade ruined, her colonial possessions dissipated. Like ancient Imperial Rome, London's crumbling ruins would be visited by the tourists of the future. Mrs Barbauld's vision, of course, was not shared by conservatives; John Wilson Croker attacked the poem fiercely in the *Quarterly Review*. One would not expect Jane Austen to have shared her sentiments either, but she would be bound to have shared her *fears*, for such ideas were circulating in Britain. And Mrs Barbauld was not against Empire, so much as illegitimate exploitation of it, a distinction hard to maintain, perhaps, but one which was made. The subtexts of *Sense and Sensibility* are manifest in the Barbauld poem: the human waste of a long, debilitating war (though Barbauld's sentiments are pacifist), the deprivation of those at home, the draining of the economy, the decline of country and empire. Barbauld's text is brilliant and complex and as ambivalent as Jane Austen's novel, but some quotations suggest its leading ideas.

> Still the loud death drum, thundering from afar,
> O'er the vext nations pours the storm of war:
> To the stern call still Britain bends her ear,
> Feeds the fierce strife, the alternate hope and fear;

Bravely, though vainly, dares to strive with Fate,
And seeks by turns to prop each sinking state.
Colossal power with overwhelming force
Bears down each fort of Freedom in its course;
Prostrate she lies beneath the Despot's sway,
While the hushed nations curse him – and obey . . .

Oft o'er the daily page some soft one bends
To learn the fate of husband, brothers, friends,
Or the spread map with anxious eye explores,
Its dotted boundaries and penciled shores,
Asks *where* the spot that wrecked her bliss is found,
And learns its name but to detest the sound . . .

Thy baseless wealth dissolves in air away,
Like mists they melt before the morning ray:
No more on crowded mart or busy street
Friends, meeting friends, with cheerful hurry greet;
Sad, on the ground thy princely merchants bend
Their altered looks, and evil days portend.[13]

Fear of an unstable war economy and a dangerously hectic commodity consumption converge. The eighteenth century is the time when commodity fetishism really got under way. One thinks of the display of the Middletons and John Dashwood.[14]

The third father figure, Hamlet's father, is a pervasive memory in the text. 'We have never finished Hamlet, Marianne; our dear Willoughby went away before we could get through it. We will put it by . . .' (Chapter 16, p. 75). Mrs Dashwood's remark is the only direct reference to *Hamlet* but the play is everywhere in the novel. It provides for that strange dreamwork structure – a kind of alternative text – which always seems to be lurking in Jane Austen's beautifully ordered writing, issuing in travesty, masquerade and dissidence. Thus the shadowy parallels make the characters and episodes come into and out of focus as they match, and do not match, the dramatic text.

The overdetermined presence of fatherless sons, the problem of the heir, and the repressed presence of war have already become a part of this discussion, and their relevance to *Hamlet* is obvious. Frenetic but secret work on Denmark's armaments 'does not divide the Sunday from the week' (I i 76), while Claudius feasts and revels. The darker side of the enjoyments pursued in the novel is more insistent when the relation with Shakespeare is established. The intensity of Hamlet's dispossession and oedipal violence gives a deeper colour to the pervasive melancholia of the male figures, and a sharper and more hysterical edge in particular to Willoughby, whose rejection of Marianne, followed by violent protestations of passion when it is too late to change anything, is akin to Hamlet's treatment of Ophelia. When we see that John Dashwood can be cast as Laertes, and the spying Mrs Jennings (it is the privilege of dreamwork to ordain changes of sex) as Polonius – 'I have found you out, in spite of all your tricks' (Chapter 13, p. 59) – both the comedy and the ironies of the novel become more intense. And Marianne's extreme grief (like Ophelia she is mourning a father and a lover), grief to the point of madness, is returned from the derivative Shakespearian conventions of feminine insanity in the sentimental novel back to its source in the original play with seering tragic meaning. Tony Tanner has rightly pointed to Marianne's grief and its excess, noting that this would have been seen as a form of madness, or allied to it, in the eighteenth century.[15]

But the perverse inventiveness of the dream structure is perhaps most apparent in the case of Mrs Dashwood. There are many matches in the novel, most oddly mismatched – Sir John and Lady Middleton, Charlotte and Mr Palmer, Lucy and Robert Ferrars, Marianne and the father figure, Brandon – but Mrs Dashwood, still young, intense and vital like her daughter, remains unmatched. Except that the text's dreamwork energies transgressively ally her both with Colonel Brandon, who, after all, is only a few years younger than she, and with the intense Willoughby, who celebrates her cottage home the day before he departs almost as if he is making love to her. Her refusal to enquire into the relationship between Marianne and Willoughby, and her own extreme grief on his departure, hint at the taboo of incest, the taboo Gertrude breaks in *Hamlet*. As a reinforcement of this Mrs Jennings and Sir John are better matched temperamentally than Sir John and her daughter. One of the effects of such taboo hints is to put a subliminal pressure on the reader which forces a recognition of the poignant sexual and social restrictions on the figure of the widow, and of unmarried women.

As important, the incest theme, recollecting Hamlet's 'A little more than kin, and less than kind' (I ii 65), suggests the question, not so much what is forbidden? as what *is* possible? What does constitute and sustain the bonds of relationship? Can the network of family connection stand for a model of society at large? What is the nature of individual *attachment* and family *connection*? These words, it has already been noticed, do searching work in this text, and it is appropriate to turn to them now.

*

The first chapter of *Sense and Sensibility* introduces such a tangle of connections and attachments, and such complex family relationships, that it is worth pausing on the first paragraph of the novel: 'The family of Dashwood had been long settled in Sussex.' The element of historical continuity is emphasized: 'for many generations . . .' And with this continuity the understanding that the family as collective entity defines and is defined by property emerges: 'Their estate . . . their residence . . . their property . . .' 'Their' is a function of ownership. Not individuals, not even biological blood relationships, constitute the family. It is an abstract concept. It has historical continuity precisely because it transcends history as a permanent entity. The family's general life is independent of the contingency of the particular individuals belonging to it. The unmarried owner's spinster sister having died, Henry Dashwood and his wife and children supply the place of carers and housekeepers. Henry is the immediate legal inheritor of the estate but the ties of affection grow up in the ten yeas of care. 'His *attachment* [emphasis added] to them all increased' (Chapter 1, p. 3). But neither legal nor affective ties seem to define the family. The estate is left only temporarily to Henry Dashwood, who is encumbered with a second wife and three penniless daughters. He can enjoy the use of the income while he is alive, but the estate passes into the hands of his son by his first wife, and thence to his son's son. Because Henry dies so soon after his uncle, there is no time to make prudent profit on the use of the estate.

The story of this betrayal is told from the point of view of the first uncomprehending shock of the Dashwood sisters and their parents. Why should the estate be left to a scarcely-known small child, not in the direct line of inheritance, in place of themselves, who had lavished affection on its owner? But the answer to this question follows from the logic of the first sentence of the novel. The small boy can perpetuate the *name* of Dashwood. This is what family means, and why it has to be patriarchal. The *daughters* of Henry Dashwood, who would presumably marry, cannot perpetuate the Dashwood name, and the name would pass out of connection with the estate. The country seat would become disconnected from the continuity of the name of its owners. The abstract being of family would be lost. In the eighteenth century, heirship strategy was bent upon maintaining the link between the family name and the family seat in perpetuity. In cases of indirect inheritance, or if women were the legatees of property, elaborate arrangements were made to preclude the loss of this tie through mobility. Name-changing by fictive kin was common.[16] Jane Austen had close personal – and probably very painful – experience of this process

17

at more or less the same age Marianne would have been when she arrived at Norland at the age of six, ten years before Henry Dashwood died (when we are told she was nearly seventeen). When Jane Austen was eight her brother, Edward, was adopted by a distant cousin of the Revd. George Austen with landed property, and his name was changed to that of the owners, Knight. In 1797 (when the novel was being revised), Edward came into possession of Godmersham Park in Kent.[17] In one sense this was an arbitrary stroke of fortune: in another way, Edward's gender determined his fate, just as John Dashwood's son comes into a fortune by virtue of his sex.

The story continues. The Dashwood sisters leave Norland. Having been imported into Henry Dashwood's home on the grounds that they are family, they leave it on the grounds that they are not. Mrs John Dashwood has gradually whittled down the material help John Dashwood feels obliged to offer by virtue of a promise to his father: 'And what possible claim could the Miss Dashwoods, who were related to him only by half blood, which she considered as no relationship at all, have on his generosity?' (Chapter 2, p. 7). True in one sense, yet exactly the same argument of distance applies to the relation between the late owner of Norland and John Dashwood's son, but is not recognized because primogeniture recognizes a boy and not a girl. The statement about 'half blood' is beautifully poised between a general statement and a belief, hardly disinterested, emanating from Fanny Dashwood's consciousness.

When Mrs Dashwood departs she carries away the handsome plate, china and linen from her former residence, prior to the ten years at Norland. Heirlooms of this kind were movable and individuals had some control over effects. It is at this point that Fanny Dashwood abandons the vocabulary of distance and chooses to emphasize the *close* relation between Mrs Dashwood, who is not his biological mother, and John. Because she thinks the superior china and plate should belong to *her*, Fanny calls Mrs Dashwood 'your mother', not 'your mother-in-law', a designation normally used to describe Mrs Dashwood's relation to John.

It is morally possible for Fanny and John Dashwood not to recognize their own extraordinary coldness because they provide themselves with convenient alibis in terms of the definition of family, which is redefined every time Fanny Dashwood demonstrates that they have no obligation to Mrs Dashwood and her daughters. The virtuosity with which she reduces the proposed gift of £3,000 to the possibility of an occasional gift of game and the transport of the (coveted) household effects depends on a linguistic and ideological move which discounts the relationship announced by the name of Dashwood in the female line and reinforces the legitimacy of a much narrower understanding of family as that which effects the concentration of wealth and the passing on of property through the male heir. Thus it is possible to present the treatment of the female Dashwoods as a form of selflessness: landed wealth does not, as it were, 'belong' to the parents, but becomes abstracted as an almost metaphysical responsibility. Like some sacred trust it is kept intact for 'our poor little boy', rather than being dissipated for the sake of sisters who are not '*really*' (Chapter 2, p. 8) sisters in any case. The narrowness of this understanding of family is inadvertently revealed by John Dashwood – who has a fatal habit of exposing his own euphemisms for what they are – as he broodingly sees that little Harry might have 'numerous family', that is, children. The male heir's progeny fall into the definition of 'family', the sisters do not.

As a result of this definition of family, the Dashwoods become 'them', outsiders: 'I would not bind myself to allow *them* [emphasis added] anything yearly' (Chapter 2, p. 10).

The assistance he thought of, I dare say, was only such as might be reasonably expected of you; for instance, such as looking out for a comfortable small house for them, helping them to move their things, and sending them presents of fish and game, and so forth, whenever they are in season. (p.10)

When John raises the question of an annuity, and then on persuasion reduces this to the occasional present of fifty pounds, he is able to depersonalize and abstract his money, which takes on the nature almost of a moral principle, by thinking of the excluded claimants as illegitimate: 'One's fortune, as your mother justly says, is *not* one's own'. Fanny remarks that the distribution of money 'raises no gratitude at all' (p. 10). Here, in an extraordinary twist of definition, she is referring to the archaic traditions of the country house in which the owner of a landed estate distributed payment in *kind* – 'presents of fish or game' – to his tenants and dependants in return for services and *deference*. Thus she has accomplished a complete reversal of the original relationship. She moves from a situation in which she and her husband are morally obliged to provide for their relations to one in which the subservient relations are expected to be obliged to *them*. Such dependants are a nuisance, and 'drains on one's income' (p. 9), belonging as they do to the days of an inefficient and wasteful distribution of resources, but above all they *owe* their landlords something.

The brilliance of Jane Austen's management of the modulation of one rhetoric of family into its opposite is consummate. And in actual fact this 'old' discourse of deference masks what has been called a new 'possessive individualism', the notion of the family estate as a form of wealth creation and investment pursued in order that profits could be used to consolidate and expand the power and influence of its owners.[18] It is this rapacious, entrepreneurial individualism as well as jealousy which emerges at the end of the conversation in chapter two. 'Your father thought only of *them*. And I must say this: that you owe no particular gratitude to him, nor attention to his wishes, for we very well know that if he could, he would have left almost everything in the world to *them*' (p. 11). Had the female Dashwoods been left the estate, the aggrandizing project to which Fanny and John devote themselves for the rest of the novel would have been foiled. And so competitive individualism is in order here, or so Fanny believes. And this kind of competition depends for its legitimacy on defining those you compete with as the enemy. The female Dashwoods have moved from being reluctantly acknowledged as 'only half blood!' (p. 8) and at least legal entities – John Dashwood describes them by the legal word 'parties', a term of which he is very fond – to hostile and threatening outsiders by the time the marital conversation terminates. By an interesting convergence of pronouns Jane Austen contrives to place the presents of game and the female Dashwoods on the same level: 'sending them presents of fish and game, and so forth, whenever they are in season' (p. 10). Lurking somewhere in this construction is the possibility that they might be conveniently exterminated, as easily as pheasants.

The conversation between John and Fanny Dashwood is the overture to the novel's profound and searching enquiry into the meaning and nature of family. By extension this is an enquiry into civil society. Are social bonds to be conceived on the model of those to be found in and between families? If the family network and its interdependencies might be the alternative to the 'egalité' and 'fraternité' of the French Revolution, how do they work? The family in this novel is a fluctuating category, sometimes defined by biology, by law, by money and by affective ties, sometimes by none of these. In a novel obsessed by relations, people are almost always described, even in the most casual allusion, through what relation they have to one another – Charlotte's uncle at Weymouth, Lucy's uncle at Longstaple near Plymouth, for instance – rather than by what they do. When Marianne's fever becomes dangerous, Charlotte Palmer goes to stay with a 'near relation' (Chapter 43, p. 260), a phrase which earlier has suggested a completely different field of meaning in her mother's broad reference to Colonel Brandon's ward: 'She is a relation of the Colonel's, my dear; a very near relation. We will not say how near for fear of shocking the young ladies . . . She is his natural daughter' (Chapter 13, p. 59). (Elinor's non-committal 'Indeed!', a reply, which presumably recognizes that she herself is not regarded as one of the 'young' ladies, is a masterly example of the polite non-response.)

What *is* a near relation? What is a distant relation? What has this to do with class and hierarchy? Where do relations stop and friends and acquaintances start? And what about strangers? 'We have brought you some strangers', says Sir John to Elinor, when he is in fact introducing his own sister-in-law and husband to them (Chapter 19, p. 91). What ties and responsibilities do these different relations – if they are different – entail? Is it really possible to think of society as an interactive network of family connections? The 'sentimental' hero of a novel which is a shadowy presence in Jane Austen's text, Henry Mackenzie's *The Man of Feeling* (1771), responds to some orphaned children deserted by their relations by saying, 'let us never forget that we are all relations'. The novel experiments sceptically with this sentimental notion, and tests and contests its assumptions. Through the cold acquisitiveness of the Dashwoods and the empty benevolence of Sir John, the other side of this coldness, the notions of connection and family 'relations' are explored. As if to be clear how artificial these 'connections' are, the two families are made to meet only as a result of John Dashwood's snobbery in London. He pushes a meeting with those titled people on the grounds that the Middletons are Elinor's relations and thus indirectly his own.

The principle of filiation is explored in the two words, 'attachment' and 'connection', words taken for granted in late-eighteenth-century society. 'Attachment' looks towards the affective world of private feeling, though it has its public implications. To form an attachment is a way of describing falling in love, but the word does not remain with this experience as the subjective feeling of the isolated consciousness. When you have formed an attachment you are never self-sufficient: to be attached is to be associated with someone else; the self is in a state of interpersonal need, and an attachment is an intrinsically social state whether it is reciprocated or not, whether it is publicly acknowledged or not. But an attachment is well on the way to declaring two people as a social unit. When Marianne refuses to countenance the possibility of a second attachment, one of her slightly irritating romantic and dogmatic beliefs, she means an affection, an affinity, likely to issue in a formal

21

bond. The word is about relationship rather than individual feeling. It is about an adhesive condition.

In some ways 'connection' overlaps with 'attachment', but it possesses a more formal and public denotation. 'Connection' is not only the public bond in which one can expect an attachment to culminate: it refers to a range of associations, formal and informal, which mark relations between and within groups and communities, including the family. Indeed, in its clustering of multiple connections between individuals, the family is the foremost and the exemplary manifestation of connection. Strangely, 'connection' implies that which is both inclusive, affirming social bonds, and exclusive, for logically if some connections are established they will preclude others. The word has social, legal, political and philosophical implications (this last will be discussed in the fourth section of my discussion).

Throughout the novel these two words are probed and probe in turn. Despite their close semantic relationship, which opens up ambiguities she is quite ready to exploit, Jane Austen makes them work for much of the time in contrary motion to one another. The private, non-contractual aspects of 'attachment' work against the more formal implications of 'connection'. On the other hand, the public, formal nature of 'connection' can literally become form without content, an impersonal social arrangement which is judged solely in terms of its pragmatic, functional purpose in forming convenient and profitable family or economic ties. 'Attachment', of course, leans to the designation, 'sensibility', while 'connection' leans to 'sense'.

Let us consider how Jane Austen creates anxiety around the word 'connection' with its public, social implications. I begin here because the structure of the novel is almost a pun on the term, a pun of a material, literal kind. For what constitutes and facilitates connections? Roads. So much of the action of the novel is made possible because journeys are possible, journeys along the improved roads which were breaking down the isolation of parish from parish, town from town, and, above all, London, the centre of civic life, from the periphery, that is Devonshire.[19] The text is organized round journeys. The topographical space is the space of connection. But the journey is also the means by which earlier structures of relationship are broken down. Once their household effects have been sent round to Devon by sea, and the female Dashwoods have entered their cottage of retirement, mimicking a persistent literary trope of the eighteenth century, the female Dashwoods expect to lead a purely local life, cut off from prior acquaintances. The circumference of their social connections is governed by the range of their walks. Mrs Dashwood has sold the carriage, and effectively their social life is static, confined to a limited topographical space, and revolves round Barton Park, the seat of their landlord and cousin. The first half of the novel is constructed serially out of successive visits and departures. The Dashwood family in Devon is at the mercy of the roads, which make or break their connections. First Colonel Brandon departs to London, then Willoughby: Edward comes and goes, not fortuitously, perhaps, complaining of the dirtiness of the roads; the Palmers, in transit, come and go; the Steele sisters, total strangers to the Dashwoods, enter as cousins of Mrs Jennings, but claim, in Lucy's words, that 'we may be very intimately connected' (Chapter 22, p. 109) with their friends. Beneath the overt social connections another, submerged, network of connections appears to exist. Despite the indications that the female Dashwoods belong to a small, socially transparent space, social and spacial relations do not actually match.

London, that nexus of connections, is at the novel's centre: the two elder Dashwood girls *are* allowed some movement at last. They go to London for the winter season, the period when the landed gentry annually migrated to town. Despite the exact topographical demarcations which separate classes in the city and the carefully guarded distinctions of the elite – the Steeles are in Holborn, Charlotte is in Hanover Square – the crisis of the novel occurs because London facilitates fresh connections and social mobility. It would only be in London, for instance, that Elinor could meet her own half-brother by accident in a shop and brush against the brother of her future husband. London frees up the rigidity of class only slightly, but enough to enable the lower-middle class Steeles to be invited to stay with Fanny and John Dashwood, ordinarily an unthinkable connection and one which is, of course, fatal, as the submerged network of relations comes to the surface. London makes and breaks connections, as the pivotal points in the novel illustrate: Willoughby's betrayal of Marianne, Brandon's revelation of his ward's daughter's seduction by Willoughby, Lucy's seduction of Robert Ferrars, all occur in London.

The latter part of the book reverses the structure of the first: virtually in the same order as the serial journeys of the first part of the novel, groups and individuals make the return journey from the centre to the periphery. First, the Dashwood girls set out, with Brandon, followed by Willoughby's frantic virtually non-stop journey of remorse and reparation: Lucy returns to Devon to boast her marriage; Edward is the last to appear at the cottage, following Willoughby, just as in the pre-London section of the narrative. The return to the periphery makes the mobility in the novel more apparent than real, but it does suggest a number of questions. How far does local life in reality depend on the manoeuvres for power and influence going on in London or elsewhere, manoeuvres which John Dashwood understands so well? Does the return to the local merely reinforce the rigidity and exclusiveness of elite society? What room is there, if at all, for connections based, not on prudential motives but on genuine affinity? This is a question the final 'connections' ask in particular: Elinor and Edward, Brandon and Marianne, end up as a quartet of connection and interdependence. Can soldier, curate and landed gentry, reinforce connections through affection or do their affiliations actually depend on possessions and wealth?

Since the Dashwoods' marital conversation first opens up questions of family, John's prudential understanding of connection is instructive. He uses the term in its classic sense when he tells Elinor of the marriage being arranged between Edward and the Honourable Miss Morton by his mother and sister: 'only daughter of the late Lord Morton, with thirty thousand pounds. A very desirable connection on both sides' (Chapter 33, p. 189). 'A most eligible connection' (Chapter 37, p. 224), he repeats regretfully, after the scandal of the revelation of Lucy's secret engagement to Edward has broken. By the same token, Lucy is a 'low connection' (p. 225), 'the connection must be impossible' (p. 225), Robert Ferrars joins in (before he succumbs to Lucy) with 'a disgraceful connection' (Chapter 41, p. 254). For John connections are entirely matters of self or family interest. In relation to Lucy the abstract, impersonal term 'connection' masks and represses the thing it is not intended to recognize, an attachment of feeling. And, because one implication of 'connection' is the pre-formed, deterministic relation, it appears to exclude altruism. Disinterest is foreign to him. He is astonished by Colonel Brandon's gift of the living of Delaford to Edward: 'Really! – Well, this is very astonishing! – no relationship! – no connection between them! – and now that livings fetch such a price! – what was the value of this?' (p. 249). Colonel Brandon is actually asserting the archaic (and superseded) values of aristocratic patronage. John cannot understand the traditional values of the landed gentry.

It is noticeable that Elinor's acerbic verbal power, which in some ways suggests a potential for embittered spinsterhood, a trait she controls in relation to others, is used unsparingly on John. 'Indeed, brother, your anxiety for our welfare and prosperity carries you too far', she remarks, pointedly reminding him of his own lack of generosity at their first meeting in London, when her half-brother invents a large legacy from Mrs Jennings for the sisters (Chapter 33, p. 192). 'You surprise me; I should think it must nearly have escaped her memory by *this* time', she says, when John unctuously remarks that Mrs Ferrars can never forget that Edward is her son (Chapter 41, p. 251).

Elinor's sarcasm is drawn by prudential and hypocritical accounts of family. John Dashwood's obsession is not simply with money: he has the developer's passion to build up his *family* like a business. His is a typical late-eighteenth-century, entrepreneurial management of the landed estate. He 'improves' his land with a greenhouse, luxury of the rich: he has enclosed Norland Common and added to his land by acquiring East Kingham Farm, a property which would be a large tenant farm, probably worked for him by a farmer who would be obliged to him as rentier: he speculates and invests in stocks, as many of the landed elite did (often in turnpike trusts, canal companies, banking, urban development and the growing industrial infrastructure). This form of capitalism gives another sense to his usage of the word 'connection'. The landed proprietor's hold on the markets provided him with a network of financial interconnections and relationships of power. The connections established by such investment spread far beyond the immediate obligations exacted by the rentier from those working his estate into the financial structure of the nation.[20] It is characteristic of John Dashwood's appropriative nature that through Elinor, using her unscrupulously to further his social connections, he makes acquaintance with the monied Mrs Jennings (who has got rich by trade) and the titled Middletons. Jane Austen never forgets this new, exploitative understanding of family, and Elinor is its major critic.

Mrs Dashwood uses the word 'connection' in John's formal sense, painfully acknowledging its meaning when she is aware that Marianne's attachment to Willoughby has come to nothing: Mrs Smith has, perhaps, disapproved of Willoughby's projected engagement to Marianne; she might 'disapprove the connection' (Chapter 15, p. 68) (because the Dashwoods are poor), and has sent him away. Mrs Dashwood's hesitant use of the word reminds one that its very formality made 'connection' prone to be used as a euphemism in a way that gave it suggestive, almost prurient, signification. As well as suggesting the pre-given, inevitably determined and thus 'natural' relation of family and class, it could be used as a circumlocution, a periphrasis for the undesirable association. The result is that it is a word which people have trouble keeping under control, even though the periphrasis itself is intended to control meaning. 'Connection' lapses into meaning disorderly, promiscuous and arbitrary relations, the very opposite in its meaning of predetermined family and social relations. John Dashwood, always the verbally clumsiest character in the novel, uses it with extraordinary ineptitude when he tries to hint that Edward's marriage to Elinor would now be acceptable to Fanny, after the revelation of Lucy's engagement to him, as the lesser of the two evils:

'That in short, whatever objections there might be against a certain – a certain connection – you understand me – it would have been far preferable to her, it would not have given her half the vexation that *this* does'. (Chapter 41, p. 251)

Most euphemistic of all, of course, 'connection' is used as a way of referring to illicit sexual relationships. Indeed, the insult John offers Elinor is precisely that this meaning is hovering in his language. It is the word Willoughby chooses when he refers to his sexual exploitation of Colonel Brandon's ward at the moment when he confesess his feelings about Marianne to Elinor at one of the climatic moments of the novel.

'A discovery took place,' – here he hesitated and looked down. – 'Mrs. Smith had somehow or other been informed, I imagine by some distant relation, whose interest it was to deprive me of her favour, of an affair, a connection, – but I need not explain myself further,' he added, looking at her with a heightened colour and an inquiring eye. (Chapter 44, p. 273)

Earlier, revealing Willoughby's liaison with his ward's illegitimate child to Elinor, Colonel Brandon uses the same expression: 'the offspring of her first guilty connection . . . I called her a distant relation; but I am well aware that I have in general been suspected of a much nearer connection with her' (Chapter 31, p. 176). The confusion of 'connection's' signification is exposed in Willoughby's vocabulary. He distinguishes a 'distant relation', a legitimate relation, from the illegitmate 'connection', but the two terms are hard to separate.

The effect of such downward slips of signification is twofold. They bring the world of formal, polite social connections and the underworld of poverty, prostitution and sexual exploitation directly into relation with one another, deconstructing the artificial, constructed world of social and sexual relations by asking, first, what the upper, social world and the underworld have in *common* with one another (for in connecting we *link* things): and second, why they should be seen as *different*, always construed as excluding one another (for we make some links and not others). Eliza, her child, Marianne and Elinor share femininity and sexual feeling – the affinity between Marianne and Eliza is one of the reasons why Colonel Brandon falls in love with her. They share financial dependence and rigorous constraint on their sexual behaviour, which is broken at a cost Eliza experiences. What creates the difference between these women is that one group has (even if only just) a support-system of family and financial connections and one has not. But the power of family is not only founded on constraint: it is built on *exclusion*. The privilege of wealth and family connections, particularly the connections of marriage, are built on the financial and sexual exploitation of an underworld and on *disowning* those connections. The introduction of the Eliza story is not a melodramatic intrusion from the novel of sentiment but points to that hidden set of connections to which polite society responds with amnesia. Willoughby's explanation for his neglect of the woman he has seduced is simply that he *forgot* to tell her where he was! 'Common sense' (Chapter 44, p. 274), he says, would have told the younger Eliza how to find him. Hardly an excuse for his behaviour. The invocation of common sense at this point in the novel makes the first word of its title resonate disturbingly if 'sense' can justify such unthinking callousness. Willoughby saves his guilt and sorrow for Marianne: 'what an hard-hearted rascal I was!' (p. 275). His selective ethics can be directed towards her because she still belongs to the upper world of connection and power.

More problematical, because it is less clear ethically and socially, is the place of the Steeles in this world of connections. They are not pleasant: Lucy is a flatterer and an unscrupulous social climber, exactly like John Dashwood. She cruelly holds Edward to his engagement, and she is happy to wound the grief-stricken Marianne with a vindictive innuendo about her loss. Vulgar, small-minded, mean, Lucy's would-be genteel language is mercilessly parodied, as fiercely as her sister's slang – 'but perhaps you may have a friend in the corner already' (Chapter 21, p. 106) – and obsession with 'smart beaux' (p. 105). Is this because Jane Austen has more compassion for those socially beyond the pale than for the invasive, thrusting, lower professional class of clerks, doctors and teachers, who merged with the upper trading classes and who constituted a threat to class divisions? Possibly. But the novel is more robust than this view suggests. The Steeles are present precisely because they *do* create a problem for the rigid world of the elite landed class. Belonging to the proliferating groups who serviced the aristocracy, symptomatic of the multiplication of intermediary classes and gradations of status, people like the Steeles were sometimes seen by contemporary commentators as the reason for the relative social stability of British society. Yet they had claims to upwards mobility and could break the pre-determined links of family connection. By what rules and codes were they excluded from some social levels? As Lucy is only too well aware, the answer is brutal: the rules of money and power. Had they been more attractive and less canny the Steele girls might have been fodder for the Willoughbys of their world. They represent an uncomfortable intermediary position between the two Elizas of the demimonde on the one hand and the two Dashwood girls, on the lowest rung of gentility, on the other. They force Elinor, always more conscious of the niceties of status than Marianne, on to the defensive: she resents Lucy's intrusiveness. In a commentary which is halfway between the narrator's voice and Elinor's consciousness, we hear of the sickening recognition that Lucy really did know Edward well, and as this recognition occurs to Elinor, so does the retreat to the boundaries and exclusiveness of family status. 'The intimate knowledge of the Miss Steeles as to Norland and their family connections . . .' (Chapter 23, p. 117): we know that Elinor is only too aware of how tenuous her immediate family's 'connections' are with Norland now. 'Their' is the possessive, which her honesty would normally prevent her from using; nevertheless these exclusive connections are erected as a barrier to the unbearable insidiousness of Lucy.

The importance of the Steele girls in the text's analysis of 'connection' is actually paramount, for it is they who are at the centre of the ironies in the novel. Far less sophisticated than her younger sister, Anne Steele actually believes the rhetoric of connection. Invited to the town house of Fanny and John Dashwood, she takes this as a sign of genuine approval and friendship, though it is actually a way of keeping the Dashwood sisters at bay and of establishing a satisfying sense of superiority over one's social inferiors. Naive, unsuspecting, trusting in the Dashwoods, she lets out the secret of Lucy's engagement to Edward, causing the pandemonium of hysteria and panic which follows, a result which is at once the great comic crisis of the novel and a critique of the values of connection. Anne takes these for real. Her ingenuousness, however stupid, is actually the result of a simple, literal good faith. Her betrayal is caused by trust. Her inability to be cynical is at once wincingly embarrassing and admirable. She cannot read the codes, which makes her both silly and moving. It is an incident which catches the reader out as well as the Dashwood household.

But in some ways the Steeles are allowed to triumph. Lucy 'gets' (her word) Robert Ferrars and moves into a world of perpetual upper-middle-class squabbles with Fanny. They are not all that different. With splendid deconstructive irony, squabbles are made to transcend class in this case. But Lucy also gets money and power. Recent historians have suggested that upward social mobility in the late eighteenth and early nineteenth century was nothing like as frequent as has been supposed, and that social divisions of considerable rigidity and intransigence were maintained, particularly between the traditional elite and those who 'came up' through trade and trading connections. If that was the case, then Lucy's triumph is all the more remarkable.[21] She does not even have the money of trade to placate the landed class whose son she snatches. No wonder she made haste to be on her way to Plymouth to boast. There are several ways of looking at her success. The conservative reading would regard her marriage as a sign of the dilution of the aristocracy by the vulgarity of trade. The more open, possibly 'Whig' reading, would remember that the aristocracy, if they are represented by Fanny and John, were vulgar enough already and that Lucy's spirited takeover is a sign of the energy of the lower-middle classes. There is also another way of looking at her. Lucy's marriage to Robert is an insouciant moment in the text, shocking and surprising everyone, including the female Dashwoods. It deconstructs the paranoia of class in the novel, and thus opens the text to a radical reading. Devastating and unconventional readings glimmer in all Jane Austen's writings and sometimes flash out with inordinate intensity, as this does.

Lucy's success also raises serious questions about the bonds of kinship as a model for social organization. How far does the definition of kinship stretch? Hamlet's remark, 'A little more than kin and less than kind', is the constant, sceptical subtext of the discourse of connection. Hamlet is speaking of the marriage of Gertrude and Claudius. He means that the breaking of the incest taboo results in an excess of kinship, transgressing the boundaries of legitimate alliance, and destroying the accepted definitions and limits of family relationship. To be 'less than kind' is the result of being 'more than kin': illicit love is one meaning of this phrase; another is that the defining characteristics of human kind as species being have been violated. In asking what a 'near' and what a 'distant' relation might be, and in enquiring what the limits of connection are, Jane Austen considers the limits of the possible, as I have said, rather than the impossible transgression (though variants of the incest theme in addition to the ones I have already mentioned shadow the text, as will be seen). For her, to be more than kin is to make specious or unfounded claims to filiation which confuse relationships; while to be less than kind is to be incapable of human generosity unless the bonds of family prompt it. But such is the instability of 'connection' that the meaning of 'kin' is always contradictory and caught in contradictions.

29

What occurs is a series of test cases of 'kin' and 'kind'ness. The very names of the novel, too few names for too many people – Dashwood, Ferrars, John (the first names of two men in the text) – failing to differentiate between people and creating ambiguity, confuse the signification of family. Fanny is exasperated when a London acquaintance assumes her name implies true sibling kinship with the Dashwood sisters and invites them to the same function: she is forced to be 'kind' to them by sending her carriage round. There are many points in the novel when unwarranted nearness of relation is used for coercive purposes, but also when the idea of the extended family is taken to such absurd lengths that it is almost meaningless. Though, ironically, Sir John's desperate search for jollity stems from the fact that 'all seemed equally anxious to avoid a family party' (Chapter 19, p. 94), he is happy to persuade the Dashwoods to dine with the Steeles at Barton Park on the disarming grounds that, 'they are your cousins, you know, after a fashion. *You* are my cousins, and they are my wife's, so you must be related' (Chapter 21, p. 102): more than kin indeed! But this stretching of the notion of family is actually specious: we know that among the reasons why Sir John has carefully chosen the female Dashwoods as tenants for his cottage is to avoid the claims on his game which might be made by other occupants (Chapter 7, p. 29). The claims of family and financial obligation converge ambiguously, as we have seen. He is both landlord and 'cousin', that most ambiguous and contingent of relations. And this connection, along with uncle, is overdetermined in the novel like a hysterical symptom.

Mrs Jennings makes the same claim of cousinship later in the novel. Since her daughter is married to a Dashwood cousin, cousinly relations with John Dashwood's family can be assumed. For Mrs Jennings's easy-going, capacious social ideas, connection is elastic, but she is not aware that John Dashwood has wondered whether she is an eligible connection, having got her money in a 'low way'! (Chapter 33, p. 193). Moreover, she is one of the few characters in the novel who does *not* assess every act on the grounds of family connection. She keeps up with her trade acquaintances, pointedly termed 'acquaintances' by the narrative voice, and nurses the sick Marianne out of pure generosity, leaving her own daughter and new-born grandson to themselves. It becomes clear that a society based on the notion of extended family connections would be a nightmare of indefinite metonymic relationship. Its network of obligation and exploitation could never be contained or limited. Such filiations encourage self-interest, privilege, bribery, patronage, unfairness and inequality – all the features of the aristocratic eighteenth-century elite which reformers termed 'Old Corruption'. Moreoever, in such a situation the artificiality of family is evident. Mrs Ferrars changes her understanding of family relationship by fiat, excluding Edward when his engagement offends her and replacing Robert as 'elder' son. The definition of family becomes virtually a matter of convenience and caprice, made to organize relations of inclusion and exclusion at will. Lucy, for instance, terms Fanny Dashwood 'your sister', not a strictly accurate description, when triumphing over her social success to Elinor, in order to demonstrate that Fanny has been sisterly to *her* and not to Elinor.

Can the notion of family be extended to servants? Mrs Jennings thinks of giving 'my Betty' to Lucy as maid if she marries Edward. What about the joy of the servants on the Dashwoods' arrival in Devon? Is the loyal Thomas, the manservant who gives such correct but confusing information on the 'Ferrars' Lucy finally marries, a part of the Dashwood family or not? It is characteristic of the deftness of this text that it asks questions about the status of servants and brothers, class and family, through the same incident. For with the Ferrars brothers we are at the heart of the critique of family: Robert appropriates his brother's fiancée and marries her; in the same way, for this is a novel in which almost everything happens twice, Colonel Brandon's brother marries the girl Brandon himself loves, Eliza. We hear that Colonel Brandon is sexually and emotionally desperate enough to plan an elopement. Brother is in conflict with brother in this text. Again *Hamlet* resonates, as we remember Claudius and Gertrude. John Dashwood, knowing how rich Colonel Brandon is, muses that he would like to be able to call him 'brother' by marrying him to Elinor. This, the appropriation of a sibling kinship his wife has denied, is the ultimate stretching of relationship in the interest of wealth and power. Brotherhood is destroyed by oedipal and prudential motives working together in this text. 'Fraternité' is no British virtue, but the lack of it suggests that something is rotten in the state of eighteenth-century England.

In truth, the text struggles with several incompatible ideologies of family connection. There is the subtle network of tradition and interest which promotes 'Old Corruption'. But there is also its possible radical alternative, there by its absence, 'fraternité'. And John Dashwood actually parodies the ideal of Christian 'brotherhood': ironically, Christianity *is* about the 'uncontained' family in which all are interdependent. This, however, is displaced by yet another understanding of 'connection' which was dissolving older connections by replacing them with a new economic interdependency based on the market, capital, and the entrepreneurial networks of free trade: for what else is free trade as understood by Adam Smith and James Mill, the dominant late-Enlightenment economists, but a metonymic network of financial exchange, links and associations? And what *is* clear is that the 'new' connections were dissolving the old moral obligations of the landed classes, a vestige of which remains in Brandon's gift of a living.

The crisis of the definition of family in the text is responding to those conditions, which exacerbate the instability of the signification of 'connection'. The pre-determined and the arbitrary, the links which include and the links which exclude, association by likeness and by difference are all suggested by the semantic field of 'connection'. 'Connection' pretends to lateral, horizontal filiations, while in fact establishing brutally hierarchical relations based on privilege and money. But perhaps its most puzzling attribute is that it is non-contractual but formal. Despite its seeming amorphousness and flexibility, connection does not change the structure of privilege or the social order: the same structures remain, but different people fill them; that is why everything happens twice in the text. Colonel Brandon and his brother, Robert, Edward, the Dashwood sisters, the Steele sisters, Eliza and her daughter Eliza, all have little room for manoeuvre despite the impression of movement in the text.

Interestingly, 'connection' was also a political term at this time, signifying neither party not interest group nor faction but alliances and networks of less definable kinds, often based on kinship and patronage, and this reflects back on the terminology of the novel.[22] There is a warrant for such meaning in the text's pointed comic reminder of the existence of political life. Haughty Mr Palmer is standing for Parliament – one of the ways the landed elite consolidated power. Charlotte comments that he is in deep trouble with the uncongenial task of making people like him. It is not clear whether he is contesting a seat (comparatively rare in the days of single nominees, and when it was unusual for boroughs to have even as many as a thousand voters) or simply consolidating his position. One of the reasons why he does not know Willoughby is that Willoughby has connections with the (presumably Whig) opposition. But in this hint of national affairs the country gentleman's assumption of automatic right to power is given an unsettling context: Mr Palmer spends his mornings playing billiards. *Hamlet*'s 'rotten' state is surprisingly elided with the 'rotten' borough.

If 'connection' dominates the novel as a mode of exploring relationships it is nevertheless in dialogue with 'attachment'. Is 'attachment' the missing affective content of 'connection'? Both, after all, are associated with the idea of linking and bonding. Should it be possible to make the two states converge, bringing about a reconciled family community and a harmonious social order? The text strives for such an aesthetic condition occasionally, but only intermittently. For as 'attachment' persuades of the value of the feelings and emotions, so by their very nature feelings require more than the romantic solipsism which is Marianne's understanding of attachment. Indeed, the critique of a narrow understanding of 'attachment' as romantic love or self-referring feeling is almost as sustained as that of 'connection'.

Attachment's one-sidedness is poignantly revealed when Elinor vindicates her capacity to feel by telling her sister of her concealed sufferings over Edward. While desiring the public 'connection' of an engagement she has been forced into private feeling alone, nevertheless suffering the public disapprobation of Fanny Dashwood and Mrs Ferrars: 'and have suffered the punishment of an attachment, without enjoying its advantages' (Chapter 37, p. 222). Even if it takes public form, as in the attachment between Marianne and Willoughby, an attachment has no public standing, sometimes not even that of true reciprocation. It is unofficial. Feelings guarantee nothing. The paradox of the 'attachment' is that it is a social passion, the desire for public union, undergone as private experience. At the intersection of internal and external worlds, it asks questions about how private and public worlds are constituted, and who has rights over them.

Characters are vicariously obsessed with the attachments of others, insisting on bringing to light imagined liaisons and secret passions and affinities, or they fiercely repress them, making the hidden experience more noticeable in the act of repression. Fanny and Mrs Ferrars on the one hand (who do not want to recognize Elinor's attachment), and Sir John and Mrs Jennings on the other (who invent attachment everywhere), are at opposite extremes. Mrs Jennings's remorseless jokes, abetted by those of Sir John, are unremitting: the heterosexual ideology of the good match and the secret passion never lets up. The more secret the passion the more public it must be. The coupling of enormous warmth and almost magnificent insensitivity in her temperament is apparent right from the start. To use the favourite word of Charlotte and her cousins, the Steele sisters, there is something 'monstrous' about her sexual laughter at the same time that it is radically demystifying. The jokes, the perpetual innuendos, constitute a massive surveillance at the same time as they let a colossal sexual energy out of – or into – the novel.

She was full of jokes and laughter, and before dinner was over had said many witty things on the subject of lovers and husbands; hoped they had not left their hearts behind them in Sussex, and pretended to see them blush whether they did or not. (Chapter 7, p. 29)

Spontaneous, affective, reaching profoundly into the emotions, occupying interior psychological space, yet requiring a social consummation, there is no doubt that 'attachment' is celebrated as one of the most intense experiences we can have. Yet its very strength is a problem. For after all, like Marianne, we can die or nearly die of it. 'Attachment', meaning a relationship between *two* people and associated with this unit rather than with the wider social ramifications of the family group, is used far less ambiguously than 'connection'. It is not necessary to dwell so extensively on the signifying networks it belongs to. Perhaps the major difficulty is the claim to *uniqueness* associated with 'attachment' together with the privileging of the private experience. 'Attachment' aligns with a form of affective individualism just as 'connection' aligns with a form of possessive individualism; it is part of the same nexus of values which was coming to validate individualist experience. And the degree to which this affective experience can be given public *expression* is always a difficulty. Willoughby, calling Marianne by her Christian name, taking her round Allenham (the occasion of many broad jokes from Mrs Jennings), publicly flaunts a private experience through his attentions to her. The problem with the 'attachment', as Marianne's dogmatic refusal to acknowledge the possibility of the 'second attachment' declares, is its refusal to acknowledge time and the insistence on its privacy. The 'attachment' is lifted out of time and into a private space. Mrs Dashwood's exaggerated respect for Marianne's emotional privacy, and her refusal to probe intrusively into the situation of the two lovers, or supposed lovers, derives from the same values. Whereas Elinor would like a shared understanding of it.

How much consent do we give to the private sphere? The real psychological and social problems of the 'attachment' occur when the question is asked, when is an attachment not an attachment but an engagement? There is another network of puns on engagement in the text, but the crucial moment of definition comes when, in the extremity of her grief after Willoughby's cruel rejection of her, Marianne asserts, 'I felt myself . . . to be as solemnly engaged to him, as if the strictest legal covenant had bound us to each other' (Chapter 29, p. 159). But bourgeois privacy does not come under the rule of law. This fatal conflation of attachment and engagement is endorsed with the legal language poignantly appropriate only to the latter: 'I wish to acquit you' (p. 158), she writes to Willoughby; 'Oh! Willoughby . . . nothing can acquit you' (p. 160), she reflects subsequently. But her absolutism and subjective certainty that she knows Willoughby's 'heart', a certainty she insists upon, are not matched by external contract, and she is forced into the terrible solipsism of privacy, that very privacy of the heart she had celebrated before the crisis occurred. At issue is the politics of privacy. It counters the externality of 'connection' but is one-sided in its turn.

The subjective absolutism of 'attachment' requires some of the formal authority of a socially recognized bond to be sustained, just as 'connection' appears to require some inwardness, some emotional authenticity, if it is not to be cold and sterile. In many ways the terms resemble one another, signifying affinities and ties which are recognized but not quite institutionalized in legal ways. But an attachment is rarely reconcilable, except with difficulty, with a 'connection', and vice versa.

But there is one bond which does not seem to need such difficult negotiation, and that is the passionate love of sisters. 'It is Elinor of whom *we* think and speak' (Chapter 34, p. 199), Marianne bursts out in defence of her sister, when Elinor has been rudely slighted at the grand Dashwood dinner party in London. This social transgression is surely endorsed in the novel, outrageous though it is by the laws of decorum. And the text has a comic resilience here which works with the deft manoeuvre of narrative form. Not all sisters can love each other quite so much: the Steele sisters, who are at the party, are a case in point. But two other 'sisters' have discovered a lasting bond at the same social event. This, the most brilliant 'match' of the novel, transcending hetero-sexual ties and the 'blood' relation of family, is the match between Fanny Dashwood and Lady Middleton. As their exhaustive discussion on the respective heights of their boys indicates, these women were made for each other. Both cold, both ambitous, they bring about the convergence of 'attachment' and 'connection' with an ease unavailable to anyone else in the novel. This courtship scene illustrates both the formalism of connection and self-regarding nature of attachment at their worst.

At the conclusion of this discussion of family, how far is it possible to understand 'sense' and 'sensibility' further? 'Sense' acquires a pragmatic and prudential colouring through being associated with those machina-tions, particularly Lucy's, which obtain money and power through connection. John Dashwood, as we have seen, adopts a policy of prudential sense in the same way. Watching the Steele sisters operating on the Middleton family, satisfying the mother's 'rapacious' need for inordinate praise of her children, Elinor finds that she 'soon allowed them credit for some kind of sense' (Chapter 21, p. 103). This register of sense, however, belongs to the high masquerade of comedy which sharpens and simplifies in the service of satire. There are other uses of the word which are not immediately satirical. We have already noticed how Willoughby darkens the words 'common sense' by referring impatiently to Eliza's deficiency. His phrase resonates with an earlier use of the same expression when Elinor speaks to Colonel Brandon of Marianne and her resolute denial of the possibility of a 'second attachment': their father 'himself had two wives' (shades of *Hamlet* again); 'A few years however will settle her opinions on the reasonable basis of common sense and observation' (Chapter 11, p. 49). It is as if both Eliza and Marianne – who are doubles of one another – lack the reality principle which enables them to deal with practical social relations. But despite Elinor's faintly superior and condescending tone, the text at this stage does not seem much interested in pursuing common sense, using the term in a workaday rather than philosophical way. The philosophical meanings of the word emerge only retrospectively by the end of the novel and will be considered later in this discussion. At the start of the novel 'common sense' is there to provide an antithesis to the sensibility and excesses of Willoughby and Marianne. It exposes the *public* display of *private* feeling and its exhibitionism. Marianne thinks it is against 'reason' to do otherwise than act openly. Elinor's understanding of reason tells her the reverse is true. Thus common sense is in opposition to both sensibility and reason. It is also in opposition to another kind of sensibility we associate with Elinor, the capacity of reflection into experience and into self. Quite different from the hedonistic sensibility of the heart, this form of introspection and thought goes far beyond common sense. This form of sensibility is almost always associated with the inner space of home and family. Not the domestic space so much as the space of retirement and contemplation, another account of family and home quite separate from the notion of 'connections' emerges primarily through the 'sensibility' of Elinor's 'sense'.

Family for the Dashwoods is where interiority is discovered and nurtured, the space where both introspection and interpersonal relations can be supported through sustaining bonds. When the Dashwood women arrive in the Devon cottage they begin by 'endeavouring, by placing round them their books and other possessions, to form themselves a home' (Chapter 6, p. 25). Home is a provisional space, whose few material possessions consist in what feeds the mind. Family, something over and above material possessions, but needing a local habitation, is a fragile arrangement for preserving the bonds of affection, mutuality, and interior life. It values thought above all: 'sense will always have its attractions for me', Elinor says of Colonel Brandon, meaning that he has a 'thinking mind' (Chapter 10, p. 45), and actually co-opting his sense into sensibility. A concept, an idea, of social existence, this form of family is as ideal and abstract, perhaps, as the 'transcendent' account of family as the preservation of name and lineage to which Fanny and John hold so voraciously, and with such self-importance. It is open to its own kind of abuse. But arguably it is the product of the humane values of sensibility.

This new consciousness of the private self nurtures and is nurtured by sensibility. Indeed, the beginning of the novel is a study in two kinds of sensibility: Elinor's and Marianne's. Both value attachment over connection and common sense. Marianne values spontaneity, openness and intensity; Elinor values reflection, scrupulousness and integrity; but both are placed in opposition to other forms of family and community in the novel. Willoughby gives a sincerely meant but bad imitation of the Dashwood values the day before he leaves their cottage for ever. Presenting the contracted space of the cottage as an endangered sanctity, the scene of virtual rape and violation, when Mrs Dashwood proposes some improvements, he is prompted to hyperbole:

And yet this house you would spoil, Mrs Dashwood? You would rob it of its simplicity by imaginary improvement! and this dear parlour, in which our acquaintance first began, and in which so many happy hours have been since spent by us together, you would degrade to the condition of a common entrance, and everybody would be eager to pass through the room which has hitherto contained within itself, more real accommodation and comfort than any other apartment of the handsomest dimensions in the world could possibly afford. (Chapter 14, p. 65)

The problem with this coupling of family and sensibility, while it provides the solution to a hard, prudential understanding of family and property, is its failure to offer an adequate account of community or civic life. The aestheticizing of sensibility and privacy is made genuinely beautiful in the text, particularly as it is an aesthetic life wrested by the family out of poverty and humiliation. The reading, the music, the walks in the wind, away from the narrow dark passage and the smoking kitchen, are truly sustaining. And yet sensibility is inward-looking.

The responsibilities of sensibility are a major preoccupation of the novel. A response to the dearth of community, there is always the possibility that sensibility may be the double of this lack rather than its true opposite. Perhaps the sensibility of the family is not a true alternative to the prudential sense of property but simply another form of possessive individualism, based on emotional rather than material acquisitiveness. This possibility is encountered in the novel, as will be seen. Certainly, the robustly superficial social life galvanized into being by Sir John – the hops, the boating trips and the incessant dinners with the Careys, Whitakers and Gilberts of his acquaintance – do not provide an adequate ground for genuine social existence. The noisy 'parties' of young people the forty-year-old Sir John is perpetually 'forming' (Chapter 7, p. 28) in quest of enjoyment are as self-absorbed as any of the self-conscious gestures to anti-social privacy which Marianne contrives. The sediment of political terminology in the language with which the hectic social activities are described – 'parties', 'forming' – suggests that these noisy upper-middle class groups are extensions of the irresponsible 'factions', of whatever political colour, into which political life could resolve. They suggest the thinning out of community and civic life. The anxiety underlying Sir John's exercise of hospitality, as he presses baskets of fruit, game and newspapers upon his relations, is disturbing. He is a man with a 'good heart', a benevolent, generous if undiscriminating figure. But Jane Austen's praise is at once approving and savage: 'and in settling a family of females only in at his cottage, he had all the satisfaction of a sportsman' (Chapter 7, p. 29). The sentence structure takes up the avenue suggested by Fanny Dashwood's reference to game: the female Dashwoods may be a species of game for this hunting and shooting man; but the momentary flicker of sexual predatoriness dies down, for we hear that their virtue is that they are *not* sportsmen, who might be entitled to shooting rights. One motive of generosity is the preservation of game. Thus with this sentence the idea of community weakens rather than strengthens. And the family of females takes on the character of a self-contained and isolated unit.

The family of sensibility's remoteness is marked by its antipathy to children. The famously acid, 'On every formal visit a child ought to be of the party, by way of provision for discourse' (Chapter 6, p. 27), initiates a critical dislike of children and indulgent parents which runs through the book. Children tear Lady Middleton's and the Steele girls' clothes; they scream and sulk and bid for attention; they are greedy and destructive. The book's response to children is so violent and intense that the animus seems almost explicable as envy and jealousy on the author's part. There may well be reasons for this antipathy to be found in Jane Austen's life, but there is a logic to the dislike of children within the text. Children are heirs, and thus a form of investment, the owners of future possessions endowed by family strategy and heirship policy. Children are instrumental for maintaining the perpetuity of the landed family. But the family of sensibility refuses this materiality as a gross denial of the true values of family, which are not based on biology but on aesthetics and ethics. Both Elinor and Marianne react with distaste to the importunate claims of unruly children.

The text's ambivalence towards the family of sensibility is suggested by the way its interiority and inner space is constantly assaulted and invaded. Willoughby, for instance, announces his presence and his sexual authority without ceremony by carrying Marianne bodily into the house.

Then passing through the garden, the gate of which had been left open by Margaret, he bore her directly into the house, whither Margaret was just arrived, and quitted not his hold till he had seated her in a chair in the parlour. (Chapter 9, p. 37)

A moment of almost lyric meditation on Elinor's part is broken into by Sir John, and the high comedy on his peremptory cheerfulness and easy assumption of intimacy (actually based on his ownership of the cottage) cannot assuage the almost physical pain with which the intrusion into interior space is presented. Sir John comes familiarly to the window rather than to the door. The passage is worth quoting in its entirety, because the modulation from inner reflection to adjustment to the intransigent demands of social life is so carefully and eloquently charted. Interior and exterior space are forcibly brought into relation with the sound of a gate closing. Up to this point Elinor has been struggling to understand Edward's behaviour, moving from 'tenderness, pity, approbation, censure and doubt' (Chapter 19, p. 91). Delicate, exact, and unusually detailed, this passage of enforced arousal from reverie is eloquent testimony to the penetrative roughness of the outside world. Willoughby's incipient sexual metaphors are as appropriate here as they were hyperbolic on an earlier occasion.

From a reverie of this kind, as she sat at her drawing-table, she was roused one morning, soon after Edward's leaving them, by the arrival of company. She happened to be quite alone. The closing of the little gate, at the entrance of the green court in front of the house, drew her eyes to the window, and she saw a large party walking up to the door. Amongst them were Sir John and Lady Middleton and Mrs Jennings, but there were two others, a gentleman and lady, who were quite unknown to her. She was sitting near the window, and as soon as Sir John perceived her, he left the rest of the party to the ceremony of knocking at the door, and stepping across the turf, obliged her to open the casement to speak to him, though the space was so short between the door and the window, as to make it hardly possible to speak at one without being heard at the other. (Chapter 19, p. 91)

Elinor's only resistance is to refuse to crane out of the window to gaze at Mr Palmer and his wife!

Psychological and social space make conflicting claims in this novel, as the responsibilities of sensibility are explored. Does the aesthetic family turn its back on other kinds of community? Fittingly enough for a family of female intellectuals, the responsibilities of sensibility are worked out through an enquiry into aesthetic matters, particularly through the literary texts of retirement and discussions of the picturesque. The following section takes up this exploration.

Section Two
Taste: Gourmets and Ascetics

The female Dashwoods appear to occupy themselves with the traditional accomplishments of the women of the leisured classes. They are pictured reading, drawing and making music. Elinor's painted screens, of course, occasion the deliberate insults of Mrs Ferrars at the Dashwood dinner. Marianne's passion for Cowper is apparent from one of her earliest conversations, when she describes Edward's dull and unexpressive reading of his poetry: 'I could hardly keep my seat. To hear those beautiful lines which have frequently almost driven me wild, pronounced with such impenetrable calmness, such dreadful indifference!' (Chapter 3, p. 15). There is a distribution of aptitude which, we shall see, is significant. Elinor paints and draws, and Marianne sings, plays and reads poetry. But what must be stressed, and what is the most important aspect of their aesthetic occupations, is the intense seriousness with which these pursuits are regarded. This seriousness differentiates the Dashwood women as a family from everyone else in the novel; for them, the new bourgeois category of the aesthetic is of the utmost importance. It is a form of *knowledge*. Lady Middleton packed in her music the moment she married. Fanny has a new greenhouse built especially for her, but that is the end of her aesthetic interests. Charlotte Palmer and the Steeles have no intellectual interests. The Dashwood dinner betrays 'no poverty of any kind, except of conversation . . .' (Chapter 34, p. 197). 'Politics, inclosing land, and breaking horses', is all that the gentlemen supply, though this is preferable to the incessant talk about children.

In a typically muted aside, Jane Austen lets us know the grounds of Lady Middleton's dislike of the Dashwood girls. They do not flatter her or her children as the Steeles do. But, more important, they have 'too much sense to be desirable companions' (Chapter 36, p. 207). Again, Elinor and Marianne are *both* associated with sense here, just as they are both associated with sensibility at other times in the novel. What disqualifies them for Lady Middleton, it is made clear, is that they are intellectual women. In a blind and prejudiced way she thinks of them as bluestockings, intelligent and critical women, who 'because they were fond of reading, she fancied them satirical: perhaps without exactly knowing what it was to be satirical; but *that* did not signify. It was censure in common use, and easily given' (Chapter 36, p. 207).

Jane Austen is implicitly allying the Dashwood sisters with the famous eighteenth-century Blue Stocking Circle, an association which included women intellectuals who gathered together for conversation, and who made a very considerable impact on high society and intellectual life in the metropolis.[1] As intellectual women, the Dashwoods put Lady Middleton on the defensive. She is thoroughly suspicious of them. And they, in their turn, are only too aware of her limitations. It is clear that their confidence and belief in themselves stem from their commitment to aesthetic and intellectual pursuits and the capacity for detachment and critique which this allows. This seriousness gives dignity to their poverty. It makes Marianne arrogant on occasion. Their pursuits are not mere accomplishments but genuine intellectual and aesthetic projects; real work. (Think how Marianne vows to undertake a massive programme of music and reading when she returns to Barton Cottage after the Willoughby crisis.) 'What a happy day for booksellers, music-sellers, and print-shops!', Edward says, when he imagines what the Dashwoods would do were they to come into unexpected fortunes (Chapter 17, p. 81). The Dashwood women – for Mrs Dashwood is included in the education of the mind – are distinctive, and perhaps distinctive not simply in this text but among Jane Austen's women figures, in being deliberately presented as thinking, articulate, and intellectually aware. Aesthetic practices give them a sense of autonomy and identity. It is therefore not surprising that some of the crucial contemporary debates around aesthetics and taste should enter naturally into their conversation. Indeed, at times the text is dense with allusion to current discussions of the principles of art and conducts a highly self-conscious exploration of the nature of the aesthetic and aesthetic experience. Because they subscribe to the view (itself a political view) that 'taste' belongs to the moral and social virtues which transcend wealth and class, legitimizing their poverty and exclusion, the *politics* of the aesthetic are crucial for both girls. The extent to which the aesthetic confirms the social order or enables a critique of it is at issue in their debates.

There are three important discussions near the beginning of the novel. The first is an ongoing debate on taste between Marianne and Mrs Dashwood and Marianne and Elinor, covering the end of Chapter 3 and the beginning of Chapter 4. The second is a tripartite discussion with Edward, Elinor and Marianne on landscape (Chapter 16) and the third is effectively an extension of this discussion, continuing with a debate on the picturesque (Chapter 18). These discussions are all instigated, directly or indirectly, by Edward. But aesthetic judgements are implicitly made in Willoughby's case also. The difference between them is considerable. It is the difference between an ethical and a psychological aesthetic, a social and an individualist understanding of taste. The qualities of sense and sensibility perhaps relate more appositely to these two male figures than to the sisters. Jane Austen is fascinated by an affective masculinity which is deeply attractive but socially ruthless. She continues an exploration of this aestheticized male consciousness into *Mansfield Park* (1814) with Henry Crawford. In just the same way as in *Sense and Sensibility*, civic and sexual issues are disclosed in the exploration of matters of art. In *Mansfield Park* these questions are explored through Humphry Repton's theories of landscape gardening. In *Sense and Sensibility* the intertextual reference is to different accounts of the picturesque, a relatively new and much disputed category of taste, in the work of William Gilpin, Uvedale Price and William Payne Knight. These are works which continued to preoccupy Jane Austen in *Pride and Prejudice* (1813). Thus *Sense and Sensibility* initiates an important exploration, which continues in the mature novels. Before we see how aesthetics are thematized in this novel, however, the environment in which the Dashwoods come to debate some of the central aesthetic texts of their culture needs to be further understood.

To retire to a cottage in a rural environment was a familiar eighteenth-century literary convention. The trope of retirement would have been recognizable in the Dashwoods' move to Devon. 'Retirement' (1782) is the title of a poem by Marianne's favourite poet, Cowper. Columella, the central figure in Richard Graves's satirical novel of the same name, which is mentioned by Mrs Dashwood in conversation with Edward, is in part an enquiry into the virtues of rural retirement.[2] Henry Mackenzie's novel, *The Man of Feeling* (1771), another text which is a presence in Jane Austen's novel, as we shall see, contains episodes which move from the rural tranquillity and decent poverty of the country scene to London and back. But there are substantial and important variations on these tropes. For one thing, the Dashwood poverty is involuntary. There is no element of choice about their move. For another, they take up the convention of retirement, which is a male choice and prerogative, as a community of *women*. The change of gender radically alters this literary convention in two ways. The women are disempowered by poverty rather than enabled by it. But on the other hand, they enter the masculine preserve of thought and meditation

43

in retirement and occupy its ground as women forced to be autonomous figures. Elinor is sharply aware of their subordination and of the way lack of money constricts their lives. She counters Marianne's romantic disdain and lack of realism about money – 'money can only give happiness where there is nothing else to give it' – with hard materialist argument: '*Your* competence and *my* wealth are very much alike' (Chapter 17, p. 80). Yet the small, contracted, vulnerable group of Dashwood women do have independence of a kind. It enables Marianne to challenge Sir John's cheerful assumption that every girl is looking for a 'conquest', for instance. How little this unconventional independence is understood is disclosed in the supremely uncomprehending reply.

Sir John did not much understand this reproof; but he laughed as heartily as if he did, and then replied,

'Aye, you will make conquests enough, I dare say.' (Chapter 9, p. 40)

To live at Barton Cottage is to see experience from the perspective of the less privileged vision. For the cottage is a trope within the trope of retirement, and Jane Austen's almost stylized allusion to it testifies to the self-consciousness and originality with which she makes literary devices work for her. For the cottage, normally a *part* of the picturesque landscape the viewer in search of aesthetic scenes would comprehend in his (and it is usually his) gaze, is the place where the Dashwoods see experience, including landscape, *from*. This literally gives them a different perspective on the landscape and aesthetic of the picturesque.

Everybody else looks *at* the cottage, not *from* it. Mrs Palmer exclaims at its prettiness; Willoughby, in an extravagant moment of sentimentality which earns some costive responses from Elinor, says that he would pull down Combe Magna if he could and rebuild a replica of Barton Cottage there, a kind of reverse 'improvement'; Robert Ferrars describes the fashionable cottage of the aristocrat playing at rural solitude. He is oblivious of the functional nature of a cottage to the poor agricultural day labourer of the times, and his advice to Lord Courtland reflects only an acquisitive pleasure in luxury and consumption: 'I advise everybody who is going to build, to build a cottage' (Chapter 36, p. 211). Jane Austen satirizes the sentimentalizing tendency among aristocrats (the Marie Antoinette factor) and even of the Dashwood family itself: as a house, she writes, their dwelling was perfectly satisfactory. As a cottage, 'it was defective, for the building was regular, the roof was tiled, the window shutters were not painted green, nor were the walls covered with honeysuckles' (Chapter 6, p. 24). In other words, this is not the idyllic English thatched cottage which, with its labouring occupants, was the subject of literary discussion and debate, mystified and demystified, from Goldsmith and Crabbe right through to the Romantic poets, either praised for its signs of agrarian contentment and simple virtue among the labouring classes or vilified as a wretched hovel, occupied by the exploited and degenerate poor.[3] Southey, Jane Austen's contemporary, nostalgically celebrated the thatched cottage a few years after the publication of *Sense and Sensibility*. The 'rose bushes beside the door' indicated an 'innocent and healthful employment', he wrote, a description which was sharply questioned by Macauley, who saw the conservative vision of an England of 'Rosebushes and poor rates' as evidence of a blind and retrograde politics.[4]

The glancing satirical remark about the cottage 'defective' in honeysuckle shows Jane Austen to be well aware of the simmering beginnings of the cottage controversy and its ideological issues as well as of the false sentiment of bourgeois-aristocratic 'retirement' conventions. While the rich built cottages the dwellings of the poor decayed in direct consequence of the French wars, as is suggested by Wordworth's 'The Ruined Cottage' (begun in 1797 and included in *The Excursion* (1814)). Margaret, another husbandless woman, lapses into despair and indifference when her husband disappears after enlisting for the French wars. The decaying cottage signifies her psychological disintegration and the decay of the social fabric: unpruned, 'The honeysuckle, crowding round the porch' (1, 715), is the first sinister sign of trouble to the visitor.[5] Jane Austen could not have known Wordsworth's poem, yet she was sharply aware of the bad faith engendered by false sentimentality about cottages and those forced to live in them. The privilege of a tiled roof is not to be taken lightly and bad fortune is always relative.

There are other intertextual hints which satirize the convention of rural idyll in poverty. 'To what purpose do we cultivate an exquisite taste and delicacy of sentiment, that only serves to make us miserable?', asks Hortensius, one of the characters in Richard Graves's *Columella*, in a discussion of the actual boredom of 'the pleasures of retirement, and a rural life'. Columella, whose nickname betokens classical pastoral, instances the gentleman who retires, but whose 'whole happiness' is in 'visiting and cards', or looking out for people travelling along the public road, almost as if anticipating Sir John's restlessness and Mrs Jennings's curiosity. *Columella* too debates the question of what constitutes a '*competence*' in retirement. In an era of upper-class luxury and the increasing tendency of the landed elite to see property as investment this is an important question because, as Elinor also sees, the idea of the competence has been relativized: of this new, aggressive seeking out of profit, a character in Graves's novel remarks, 'It shocks me to observe, how small a part of mankind are able to set bounds to their avaricious desires'.[6] Retirement cannot escape from the money society.

What kind of socially sustaining experience can be gained from the life of retirement and aesthetic contemplation? Do their values betray a truly civic or civil life, marking a turn from a public understanding of civil society to the politics of privacy? What are the responsibilities of sensibility? To see how Jane Austen takes up these questions it is necessary to look more closely at the ethics and economics of landscape appreciation in the novel, and to the dialogue between Elinor and Marianne about it.

The location of the new dwelling is very carefully described. Since it is rare to find Jane Austen describing scenery, it is worth pausing on her description. The West Country landscape of Barton Valley 'was a pleasant fertile spot, well wooded, and rich in pasture. After winding along it for more than a mile, they reached their own house' (Chapter 6, p. 24). The 'situation' of the house, which was 'good', is further described.

High hills rose immediately behind, and at no great distance on each side; some of which were open downs, the others cultivated and woody. The village of Barton was chiefly on one of these hills, and formed a pleasant view from the cottage windows. The prospect in front was more extensive; it commanded the whole of the valley, and reached into the country beyond. The hills which surrounded the cottage terminated the valley in that direction; under another name, and in another course, it branched out again between two of the steepest of them. (Chapter 6, pp. 24–5)

With delicate topographical precision the landscape comes into being. It is a mixed agrarian landscape of timber, pasture (for cattle and sheep) and crops (signified by the designation 'cultivated'). It is enclosed by hills and subordinated to the village (as also to the country seat, Barton Park), which is above it, at the back. Yet it opens out on to an expansive prospect at the front. In its valleys and wooded hills, declivities and rising ground, it is subtly expressive of feminine symbols. At the same time it is scrupulously attentive to the social. The 'views' from the cottage are split. Behind it is the village, in front of it is the expansive natural landscape stretching far into the distance. One view looks to community and hierarchy, the other celebrates the privacy of the individual eye which 'commanded' a view of the whole valley. There is a hint of a will to power and control over space and territory as the gaze attempts to encompass an expansive scene. Marianne experiences a similar split vision, though one of a far more schizophrenic kind, when she describes the illicit visit to Allenham made with Willoughby on the event of the cancelled excursion occasioned by Colonel Brandon's sudden departure. She speaks of one 'remarkably pretty sitting room' (Chapter 13, p. 61):

It is a corner room, and has windows on two sides. On one side you look across the bowling-green, behind the house, to a beautiful hanging wood, and on the other you have a view of the church and village, and, beyond them, of those fine bold hills we have so often admired. (p. 61)

The pleasure ground and the hanging wood on one side, bespeaking the private pleasures of the rich, the church and the village on the other, bespeaking the symbols of community and religious authority, disclose a more extreme division than that expressed by the topography of the cottage, but it is structurally the same. Marianne implies an ownership of village, church *and* the expansive prospect, as she considers the view from the Allenham window. The topographical ordering round the cottage is less aggrandizing, and in this sense more realistic. It does not presuppose that the Dashwoods are in control of their environment.

Through these exquisitely scrupulous visual details the text seeks to explore the ethical and political significance of the aesthetics of retirement. The Dashwoods have not chosen the split vision induced by the situation of the cottage ground, but they can choose to intensify the split between the social and the individual, as Marianne's experience suggests, or they can choose to mitigate it, as Elinor's experience will show. But neither choice is simple. And, to use a term overdetermined in the novel, the 'connection' between the social and individual, public and private, seems to have been lost.

The complexity of the Dashwood choices is mediated through allusion to a popular writer on the picturesque landscape, William Gilpin. At first it even seems as if Jane Austen's description is mimicking the language of his many tours through England in the late-eighteenth century. Gilpin's *Observations on the Western Parts of England* (1798) includes a critical account of a view near Exeter, a view which Jane Austen's prose seems almost labouring to correct, making ideal what Gilpin had seen as deficient.

From Exeter to Honiton we passed through a rich country, yet somewhat flatter than we met with on the western side of Exeter. We found, however, here and there, an eminence, which gave us a view of the distances around. At Fair-Mile-hill, particularly, a very *extensive* view opened before us; but nothing can make it pleasing, as it is *bounded* by a *hard edge*. A distance should either melt into the sky, or terminate in a soft and varied mountain line.[7]

The landscape of the novel indeed 'terminated' in a line of hills, as the valley branches under another name.

This artful correction draws attention to the strangeness of Gilpin's position. For while he insists that the beauty and variety of the natural scene can never be rivalled by art, his criteria for the 'good', picturesque landscape are precisely those kinds of beauty 'which *would look well in a picture'*.[8] In making the landscape into that which looks well in a novel Jane Austen is reminding us that experience, far from being unmediated as Gilpin suggests, is perpetually reconstructed by the perceiver. Gilpin is perfectly happy to think of the artist as adding to or subtracting from a scene to give it more 'consequence', as he put it in his *Observations on the River Wye* (1770).[9] But for him the artist and viewer are exactly alike in their ability to select and order experience at will, seeking out what is pleasurable to the eye. Mediation is unimportant to Gilpin because his stress is on aesthetic *experience*, which can be gained either directly or through pictures. Pictorial elements might provide the criteria for pleasurable order but the status of both experiences is the same even if the actual, first-hand experience of landscape is preferable to art. To gain *actual* picturesque experience Gilpin will seek out the 'eminence' or vantage point which will best enable him to control and organize the visual elements he requires. The power of the eye – 'command' – as Jane Austen knowingly puts it, is all-important. Gilpin complains of overbuilding in Devon, for instance, and selects out human habitation from the prospect. The selective eye censors as it views. So that near Taunton, the view from 'high grounds is very grand'. He thinks of the prospect as direct, unmediated experience, but it is not:

composed on one side of Barnstaple-bay, and on the other of an extensive vale; the vale of Taunton carrying the eye far and wide into its rich and ample bosom. It is one of those views which is too great a subject for painting. (*Observations on the Western Parts of England*, 175)

Viewing the picturesque is actually about power. John Barrell has argued that the controlling eye betokens ownership of the wide expanse of enclosed land.[10] The view or prospect is seen from a fixed position and the eye sweeps immediately from horizon to foreground and back. This is a way of controlling nature and subjecting it to civilized order. Nature, for the Whig and mercantile elements of eighteenth-century society in particular, was there to be conquered and to yield up riches. One can add to this that in Gilpin's description the eye becomes sexualized as it is carried into the bosom of the vale. Strikingly, however, it is impossible for the Dashwood women to establish this perspective. Divided though their vision might be between community and privacy, the appropriating, individualistic gaze is not available to them in the form Gilpin prefers. The 'prospect' is not seen from an 'eminence' or from 'high grounds', and it is not 'extensive', only *'more* extensive' than the view behind. The 'prospect' is actually seen from below, seen from a *restricted* perspective, not from the wide expanse of enclosed land indicative of unimpeded possession. And it is the prospect, the syntax allows, not the eye, which commands space. Landscape is independent of the self. In fact Jane Austen's passage challenges Gilpin's picturesque perspective and its values of control and command. If the women take over the masculine prerogative of retirement and aesthetic speculation, they do so, if not to create a feminized picturesque, at least from another position altogether, a position which relinquishes the assumption of control. It is also a position which recognizes selection and mediation as inevitable. Thus it recognizes that the response to landscape is ideological.

It appears to be easier for Elinor to recognize the Barton perspective than for Marianne. It is not simply that she is aware of social obligations and dependencies in a way that Marianne refuses. Marianne struggles to regain the lost high ground, though rather to transcend her powerlessness than to regain power. She is described as possessing 'a life, a spirit, an eagerness, which could hardly be seen without delight' (Chapter 10, p. 41), and it is this energy which impels her, for instance, to challenge a rainy day and to seek the fresh air on the high downs surrounding the cottage on the day of the fatal fall down the hill. The iconography of this episode is crucial to Jane Austen's critique of picturesque experience. Marianne's favourite Cowper speaks of the customary move to high ground:

> Now roves the eye;
> And, posted on this speculative height,
> Exults in its command.
> (*The Task*, Book I, 'The Sofa', 288–90)[11]

In like fashion, the girls ascend the hill 'rejoicing' (Chapter 9, p. 37), but Marianne never reaches the 'command' of the summit. Warning against impetuosity, Cowper writes, 'Descending now (but cautious, lest too fast) / A sudden steep . . . We mount again' (I, 266–7, 271). The text fails to accept Cowper's admonition and stages the fall he warns against. This fall from the overview, from control and power, can also be staged as a moral and sexual fall, for after all, Marianne falls into Willoughby's arms. But its significance is wider. Marianne is quite literally precipitate, 'too fast' in many senses, perhaps. Her fall dislodges her not only from a 'command' of experience but also from a fixed position. Unlike the self-stabilizing and self-protective Cowper, her volatile energy disrupts the order of the picturesque even while she feels that it is with the picturesque that she belongs emotionally. The novel mounts a double critique. The omniscient, possessive, exploitative power of the overview is unacceptable to it. At the same time, the uncentred emotions of the perspective from below lead to incoherence, fragmentation. Fragmentation is constantly Marianne's problem, created by the very spirit of life which makes her so attractive.

The first encounter with Edward, who has come unexpectedly to visit Barton, continues the exploration and critique of the picturesque. This is what may be termed the dead leaves episode. After an embarrassed silence the newly-reunited group embarks upon the scenery as a topic of discussion. Marianne enquires about Norland. Elinor, with some sarcasm, responds to Marianne's raptures at the thought of the autumn landscape in Sussex. 'It is not everyone ... who has your passion for dead leaves'. The same bathos occurs when Edward seems impervious to the beauties of the Devon landscape, but remarks that, 'these bottoms must be dirty in winter', and reiterates his complaint about the dirty lane. 'How strange!' said Marianne to herself as she walked on (Chapter 16, p. 77).

Down in the valley, not up in the hills this time, the position is commensurate with the perspective from below as well as the bathos that comes of a confrontation between practical sense and self-indulgent romanticism, or sensibility. But again, the issues lie deep. Marianne thinks of the 'transporting sensations' induced by the leaves 'driven in showers about me by the wind!' (p. 77). There *is* lyricism here intertwined with the satire, and it derives from another poet, this time Thompson's *The Seasons* (1726–30). In 'Autumn' Thompson describes a storm in which, 'Strained to the root, the stooping forest pours/A rustling shower of yet untimely leaves' (320–21).[12] But Marianne takes some things from Thompson and not others. The intensity and violence of autumn weather is celebrated in the poem, but it is the cause of immense destruction, ruining the harvest and killing animals and people alike. Marianne's self-absorbed sensibility actually becomes a form of imperviousness to social existence. The other side of sensibility is hardness of heart, as the allusions to hunting in Thompson's poem suggest. Willoughby hunts, as Edward does not take long to guess. Earlier he had challenged her to explain why hunters should be a necessity: 'But most people do,' she replies carelessly to his 'Every body does not hunt' (Chapter 17, p. 80). This betrays an extraordinary willingess to accept conventional customs which Marianne's unconventionality in other respects would surely deplore. She forgets the powerful attacks on aristocratic blood sports in Thompson's poem which follow directly after her allusion to his autumn leaves: 'This falsely cheerful barbarous game of death,/This rage of pleasure . . .' (384–5). Sensibility is incoherent, fostering feeling on one hand and destroying it on the other, cultivating the heart, destroying the bonds of communality with social beings and with living things.

When Marianne points out the beauties of Devonshire to Edward she betrays that same selective vision we have seen at work in Gilpin's *Observations*.

Here is Barton Valley. Look up to it, and be tranquil if you can. Look at those hills! Did you ever see their equals? To the left is Barton park, amongst those woods and plantations. You may see one end of the house. And there, beneath the farthest hill, which rises with sudden grandeur, is our cottage. (Chapter 16, p. 77)

It is the grand scene that matters. The evidences of cultivation, labour and human habitation, other than their own and their landlord's, do not appear in her description. Of course, there is poignancy here: Marianne is attempting to show Edward that they are happily settled after the disruption of the move. Nevertheless her picturesque language obeys Gilpin's prescriptions. He specifically repudiates grounds laid out by art or 'improved by agriculture' as elements of the picturesque. 'Manufactured scenes' and 'artificial appendages', as he calls them, that is, scenes containing evidence of human labour, destroy picturesque experience. Milkmaids and mowers, hedgerow elms and furrowed fields may be just acceptable in poetry (he instances Milton's *L'Allegro*), but they do not constitute the true content of the visual material which would look well in a picture. He reserves his most intense disgust for the hay field and the land, which has been 'disfigured by the spade, the coulter, and the harrow'. Turning to the Isle of Wight, near to Jane Austen's homeground, and included in his West Country tour, he writes:

. . . and of all species of cultivation, cornlands are the most unpicturesque. The regularity of corn-fields disgusts; and the colour of corn, especially near harvest, is out of tune with almost everything else (*Observations on the Western Parts of England*, 255).

The physical language of taste here – 'disgusts' – is strong. The taxonomy of the aesthetic landscape deliberately excludes any element of labour, which induces nausea, from its wholly artificial nature. This is the ground of both Elinor's and Edward's dissent from Marianne's ideology of the picturesque. Edward returns to the theme of the picturesque after he has looked at the village, and what he offers her is a virtual reprimand. The two passages in which he challenges the picturesque taxonomy deliberately introduce the rural economy into the landscape. They are important, and worth quoting in full.

Edward interrupted her by saying, 'You must not inquire too far, Marianne – remember I have no knowledge in the picturesque, and I shall offend you by my ignorance and want of taste if we come to particulars. I shall call hills steep, which ought to be bold; surfaces strange and uncouth, which ought to be irregular and rugged; and distant objects out of sight, which ought only to be indistinct through the soft medium of a hazy atmosphere. You must be satisfied with such admiration as I can honestly give. I call it a very fine country – the hills are steep, the woods seem full of fine timber, and the valley looks comfortable and snug – with rich meadows and several neat farmhouses scattered here and there. It exactly answers my idea of a fine country, because it unites beauty with utility – and I dare say it is a picturesque one too, because you admire it; I can easily believe it to be full of rocks and promontaries, grey moss and brush wood, but these are all lost on me. I know nothing of the picturesque . . . I like a fine prospect, but not on picturesque principles. I do not like crooked, twisted, blasted trees. I admire them much more if they are tall, straight and flourishing. I do not like ruined, tattered cottages. I am not fond of nettles, or thistles, or heath blossoms. I have more pleasures in a snug farmhouse than a watch-tower – and a troop of tidy, happy villagers please me better than the finest banditti in the world.' (Chapter 18, pp. 84–5)

Edward in fact knows a great deal about the picturesque. Not only does he virtually quote Gilpin on the soft medium of the melting horizon; he also cunningly conflates Gilpin's picturesque with that of Uvedale Price, who thought very differently on the picturesque experience, and he alludes to Cowper's 'Yardley Oak' (Was this the poem Marianne thought he read so expressionlessly earlier at Norland?) Elinor is right to say that he is taking up an extreme position, as dogmatic, if not more dogmatic and self-righteous – and certainly more pompous – as that of Marianne. Consummately, the text allows his masculine certainty and aggression to make Marianne seem momentarily vulnerable, and shows up the irony of a dispossessed young woman who uses the aristocratic language of taste to console herself for loss and grief. Her retreat is poignant: she agrees that 'jargon' is an affectation; but 'sometimes I have kept my feelings to myself, because I could find no language to describe them in but what was worn and hackneyed out of all sense and meaning' (p. 85).

Edward puts a rival ideology, a rival aesthetic, against Marianne's aristocratic individualism. He finds beauty and utility united in the landscape. Indeed, beauty is utility. Beauty is an effect of functionalism, the result of good economic management. Harmony, order and the prosperous exploitation of the land come about together, producing 'rich meadows', 'neat farmhouses' and troops of 'tidy, happy villagers' (p. 85). Edward is here dissociating himself from the aristocratic values of Burke, who held that beauty was never in alliance with utility, and associating himself instead with a growing middle-class interest, the farming interest. This is a practical social theory in that it is a belief that efficiency and rational order become aesthetically pleasing because they are beneficial to all social orders. The well-managed landscape displaces the picturesque landscape. This pragmatism has radical and utilitarian overtones, and it is true that philosophical radicals such as Mary Wollstonecraft and William Godwin also adopted a functionalist account of the beautiful at this time. Two kinds of pragmatism converged, but Edward's is relatively conservative. The farming classes, required to produce increased food supplies to service troops in France and a growing population at home, embarked on a period of rationalization, as farms were expanded through enclosure, and methods of cultivation were mechanized. The economic principle of utility was important to them. Expansion often occurred under the auspices of the landed estate (as John Dashwood's assiduous purchase of farmland suggests) but a self-confident, farming middle class also emerged.[13] It is this with which Edward identifies, asserting practical utility over redundant aestheticism. It is an entrepreneurial utility, but tempered, or so he presents it, with sense and rational benevolence towards the agricultural labourer. And hunting is not on its agenda.

But Edward is a potential clergyman, we learn, likely to serve such agricultural communities and to think the best of his masters. His view constitutes a powerful critique of Marianne's position rather than being the ideal solution to the problem of aesthetic experience and social existence. For by collapsing beauty into utility he produces a highly prescriptive account of it, as prescriptive as anything in Gilpin. And what aesthetic is likely to be meaningful if it produces 'no language to describe' the feelings?

Edward feminizes and eroticizes the picturesque in an exaggerated way in order to banish it. Marianne is the unfortunate recipient of a double designation. On the one hand she is associated with a voracious aristocratic individualism, and on the other she belongs to that dangerous category of the feminine radical. In neither case does she fit in with Edward's masculine paradigm of the natural landscape ordered by cultivation. Here is where the relevance of the allusions to Uvedale Price can be seen. The satire on Price's ideas becomes more apparent in the second speech addressed to Marianne, though the greyness and darkness of the landscape described earlier suggests the tones of gloomy half light appreciated by Price. In particular, the blasted trees, the tattered cottages and the ruined, derelict landscape are all features associated with Price's picturesque. What is their significance?

In one sense Price's arguments are concerned with rather legalistic quibbling about what falls into the categories of the beautiful and the picturesque, but we have to see what cultural meaning could be attributed to those now remote categories to see why they became important. It is Price's intention to rescue the picturesque from aristocratic individualism. The picturesque for him is an experience which no longer presupposes the power and ownership of the gaze. It falls as a midpoint between the extremities of the melting passivity of beauty on the one hand and the aggressive appropriation of power which betokened the sublime on the other. Discrete details seen in isolation, details which *arouse*, are its essence. The overview is relinquished in favour of the challenge of the isolated, discrepant detail, the detail which cannot be accommodated to norms. That is why the picturesque can be ugly. An uninitiated friend in Price's *Dialogue* on the picturesque and the beautiful asks innocently why the picturesque should be ugly, and instances the oak: 'its trunk a mere shell – its bark full of knobs, spots, and stains – its branches broken and twisted, with every mark of injury and decay'. The answer is that this experience lies between the extremes of monotony (or beauty) and harshness (or the sublime): it consists in 'the grateful medium of grateful irritation, which is called beauty, or picturesque beauty'.[14]

Irritation, a term often associated with Marianne in the days of her heartbreak, denotes the capacity of susceptibility or excitability, a response of the nerves and mind to stimulus. The anomaly of the picturesque detail, its failure to fit in with cultural, ethical and social paradigms, or its capacity to arrest and surprise, is what makes it important for Price. His is an early theory of defamiliarization, but for him this defamiliarization does not simply shock or surprise. It provokes curiosity, the desire to know. This is a voyeuristic, insatiable curiosity. Later writers exploited this erotic intensity and commodified it. Jane Austen returned to this aspect of the picturesque in *Mansfield Park*, just as she expanded on the subversiveness of the picturesque as a category in *Pride and Prejudice*. But for Price as well as being the instigator of desire, the picturesque is also the source of our questioning and challenge to experience. One could think of the picturesque as provoking a vital epistephemilia, or the drive to know, which literally keeps us alive, biologically and intellectually. Elsewhere Price claimed that the picturesque is connected with political independence and the capacity of people and societies to change.[15]

The abruptness and irregularity of the picturesque, which causes the eye both to wander and wonder, is central to picturesque effect. The breaking of the undulating line and smooth curve conduced to that breaking of expectation, which is crucial if 'grateful irritation' is to be activated. The natural, as John Barrell has remarked, is no longer under the control of civilized order. Moreover, the natural elicits 'unnatural' categories.

Their [tree] forms are indeed so sharp and broken, and they are often so destitute of foliage, that a person used only to full and swelling outlines of rich vegetation, would scarcely know them to be trees. These last, however, have frequently a grand, generally striking and peculiar character; but when we call such broken, diseased and decaying forms, (and, I may add, the colours that accompany them) beautiful, either in reality or imitation, we clearly speak in direct opposition to nature; for it is just as unnatural to call an old, decaying, leafless tree beautiful, as to call a withered, bald old man or woman by that most ill-applied term.[16]

The picturesque, Price emphasizes, is aberrant, but necessarily so. A typical picturesque landscape, the strong landscape of Salvator Rosa rather than of Claude, arouses a range of questions. His exemplary landscape suggests what these are: like Gilpin's, it is a 'real' landscape, but it is very different from his:

In a dark corner of it [a common], some gypsies were sitting over a half-extinguished fire, which every now and then, as one of them stooped down to blow it, feebly blazed up for an instant, and shewed their sooty faces, and black tangled locks. An old male gypsy stood in the entrance, with a countenance that well expressed his three fold occupation of beggar, thief, and fortune teller; and by him a few worn out asses: one loaded with rusty panniers, the others with old tattered cloaths and furniture. The hovel was propt and overhung by a blighted oak; its bare roots flaring through the crumbling bank on which it stood. A gleam of light from under a dark cloud, glanced on the most prominent parts;

the rest was buried in deep shadow ... they talked in raptures of every part; of the old hovel, the broken ground, the blasted oak, gypsies, asses, panniers, the catching light, the deep shadows, the rich mellow tints, the grouping, the composition, the effect of the whole; and the words beautiful and picturesque were a hundred times repeated. (102)[17]

Price is fully aware of the satirical possibilities in his scene of avid aesthetes, and fully aware of the aspect of melodrama which it possesses. But the implied aesthetic questions are serious. The eye is intended to have its gaze dispersed over the landscape, restlessly moving from part to whole and from whole to part, never resolving its position. It is a temporal movement rather than the spatial experience such as we find in the visual relations opened up in a Gilpin landscape or the landscape of utility described by Edward. As the scene is split up into its component parts, the light, the panniers, the hovel and the oak are decomposed, as it were, and given no principle of relationship. Yet the elements of the scene *do* belong together, and we are forced to recognize not only that it is a constructed, culturally made 'composition', but ask ethical and social questions as well as purely aesthetic ones: indeed, these are incorporated into the meaning of the aesthetic. Common land, the gipsy as social outsider (here the equivalent of the 'banditti' beloved of Salvator Rosa), his non-Eurocentric blackness (Price has a long aside on the aesthetic and cultural meaning of European whiteness); his moral nature, the decayed hovel, the meaning of the asses and loaded panniers, all these make insistent demands on the picturesque vision. The eye and mind work by association and through affect to order this experience. Perhaps, since this depends on arousal and desire, one would call these the aesthetics of 'attachment', the word so frequently associated with Marianne.

The aesthetics of attachment would persuade one to ask questions about enclosure, about social and economic exclusion, about ownership and property, and the strange parody of commodity circulation embodied in the tattered clothes and furniture carried on the back of the ass. It is a scene of lawlessness which strangely parallels the self-preservation and opportunism inherent in economic individualism.

Above all the blasted oak would be an overdetermined cultural signifier, working overtime here. Timber, carefully cultivated and commercially exploited is one of the mainstays of the landscape of utility – hence Edward's repugnance for the dead tree. But the oak (the mainstay of the British Navy in the form of ship's timber) belonged also to the iconography of nation. This was at its most triumphant in Pope's celebration of the oaks in *Windsor Forest*: 'While by our oaks the precious loads are born, / and realms commanded which those trees adorn'. The oak of England for Pope is the reassuring sign of the 'Peace' and 'Plenty' which are brought about 'naturally' because 'a *Stuart* reigns'.[18] The peace of Utrecht, Tory and Stuart hegemony, economic abundance, Pope makes all these follow from the ordered landscape of Windsor Forest, itself the epitome of the aristocratic picturesque. Cowper's 'Yardley Oak', written in 1791, which meditates on the decay of the oak and the possibility of its survival is by implication a meditation on his own insecure constitution and mental stability and by extension that of the Hanoverian state. Its hinted presence and the allusion to Price's scene in *Sense and Sensibility* compounds the awkwardness of the questions being asked through the picturesque aesthetic in the novel: 'The hovel was propt and overhung by a blighted oak; its roots flaring through the crumbling bank on which it stood.' The blighted oak now hints at the blighted British Navy at war: England in the 1790s, a shaky Hanoverian dynasty, war and a war economy, poverty, want. No wonder Edward's landscape of utility wards off the blighted oak, the death of the father, the decay of nation.

Marianne's enthusiasm for the affective picturesque, with its irregularities and anomalies is an unwonted 'irritation', as Price would have it, to those who wish for a more composed and less undermining way of life. The politicization of the affective picturesque, the aesthetic of sensibility, makes her a threat, a danger. Her presence implies change, disruption, to many in the novel, and not least to Elinor and Edward. But perhaps the most difficult aspect of her life is her failure to distinguish the aristocratic aesthetic of ownership and the overview and the more radical, subversive, affective picturesque with both of which she aligns herself. This is not surprising, because Edward conflates the two, as we have seen, but in Marianne's case the contradictions of the two picturesques are damaging, and contribute to that split consciousness and divided self, which the text hints at through her double vision, the two windows of Allenham.

So far the trope of retirement, the figure of the cottage and the social and ethical values implied in different theories of the picturesque have been considered. Jane Austen makes scrupulous discriminations when introducing these conventions and debates into her text. The Dashwood women are both brave and vulnerable as they make their claims to the male prerogatives of debate, thought and aesthetic experience. They will not be the objects of any of these discourses but enter into them as participatory intellectuals. But the perspective of subordination and enclosure which their experiences are governed by necessarily makes their intellectual life a different thing from male discourse. Gradually, as the text explores the ethics and politics of taste through that great new category of enlightenment thought, the aesthetic, ideological fissures and tensions appear. The responsibilities of sensibility are not simple. Elinor and Edward prefer the aesthetics and politics of stability, the managed landscape which issues in the middle class rationale of the beauty of utility and the utility of beauty. If they represent sense rather than sensibility at this stage in the novel, it is sense which is hosted or generated by sensibility itself. Marianne, on the other hand, favours the aesthetic of affect and psychological intensity. Her experience is fragmented because she adopts two picturesques. The first is the aristocratic aesthetic of possession and power, where the viewing eye dominates or 'commands' high and low ground alike. It is a feature of both Whig and Tory experience. Though perhaps the difference is that the Tory, as in Pope's poem, posits a 'natural' affiliation between land and human society, as the corn tempts the reaper's hand, while the Whig sees the natural world as that which can be made to yield up its riches. Willoughby the hunter is certainly a plunderer of the natural. On the other hand, Marianne is attracted to the aesthetic of critique and interrogation manifested in a middle-class aesthetic very different from that of the beauty of utility. Price's theories have a radical potential because the aesthetic effect depends on a technique of destabilization. One of these destabilizing features is the suggestion that the 'natural' itself is an artificial category, and this makes for Jacobinical or revolutionary tendencies, as Marilyn Butler has noticed.[19] Though it must be remembered that the idea of the utility of beauty was also adopted by middle-class radicals, it was easier to co-opt utility in the service of order than it was to control the irregular and fragmented picturesque of 'grateful irritation'. The idea of utility is actually an attempt to masculinize beauty, moving it away from the sensuousness and passivity with which it was traditionally associated. On the other hand the affective picturesque could be made erotic and associated with femininity. It is undoubtedly questioning and challenging. It produces 'irritation': but at key moments in the novel its values are affirmed.

For despite Marianne's contradictory state and dangerous potential, and despite Elinor's excessive composure and restraint – aesthetically they are like the difference perceived in discussions of taste between Claude and Salvator Rosa – neither Marianne nor Elinor are condemned for living the life of aesthetic feeling. Nor are their experiences wholly assimilated to a masculine regulation of taste. Elinor draws,

Marianne sings and plays: sound and vision, aural and optical experience, all this is welcomed by the text and celebrated as the source of an ethical integrity and aesthetic sense which makes the two elder Dashwood sisters different from other people. Why should these skills be important?

One can begin with Elinor's drawings, which are pinned up in the new parlour, admired by Charlotte, loved by Marianne and denigrated by Mrs Ferrars. We are never told of their content, but it sometimes seems as if Elinor draws to rescue herself from depression, even neurosis, as she struggles with her hidden sense of rejection, Lucy's taunts and Marianne's anguish. It may seem strange that she is allowed to be a painter and graphic artist when she lavishes so much criticism on the psychology and politics of picturesque experience. But her art perhaps continues the dialectic of the picturesque. For, whether they thought picturesque elements were inherent in landscape or imposed on it by the mind, eighteenth-century commentators all agreed that the artist made an act of selection. Even Gilpin, for instance (the least self-conscious of commentators), allowing that picturesque beauty is that which would 'look well in a picture', sees as a consequence that the artist will be 'confined by the rules of picturesque composition'. He is confined by the compass of 'inch, foot, and yard'.[20] The artist who claims that his art can equal the natural picturesque might argue that just as a landscape seen through 'the pane of a window' is pleasing, so a picture constructed by the same conditions can also be pleasurable. Gilpin seems unaware, as has been said, that both eye and painting mediate experience, ordering, shaping and selecting. Other theorists were not so naive. William Payne Knight believed that there was nothing 'there', as it were, except what was taken back to nature from the viewer. Elinor herself seems deeply aware of the mediating power of art, always selecting, always adjusting to the external. It is significant that her meditations on Edward's inexplicable behaviour occur at the drawing-board. Her art does not raise the issue of representation so much as the process and nature of selection and accommodation which goes on continually as the artist attempts some correlation with the external world. This is the painterly equivalent of Elinor's often caustic reminders to others of the exacting discipline of the reality principle. The draftsman requires a referential grid. Nevertheless, if the draftsman, or draftswoman, learns techniques of judgement, this mediation is not founded on power and 'command' of the eyes. Representation becomes a matter of seeing relationships. But do we impose meaning or see it?

It is in their chosen art that the two girls differ most. Elinor's willing subjection to restraint is a paradoxical way of gaining control of her experience. Marianne, on the other hand, prefers an art with less referential content. Its value for her and for others is the psychological effect of its expressive possibilities. It was generally agreed in the eighteenth century that music, as 'sentimental expression', as Payne Knight termed it, appealed to the 'affections', to the emotions which responded to its vibrations. As 'the melody of inarticulate sounds', music can excite ideas, but more often, like poetry, it appeals to the feelings and sensations.[21] Nevertheless Marianne's music is very much a public, social act. She and Willoughby play and sing, but she also entertains at Barton Park, bewitching Colonel Brandon. Expressive form does presuppose listeners: music is the release of feeling in performance even though it can become a private exercise. Expressive form perhaps circumvents that painful sense of the limits of language, which Marianne experiences: the sense that she *has* no language except the pre-given formulas of picturesque categories.

Two accounts of taste are present in the novel, one leaning to Marianne's expressive aesthetic and one to Elinor's understanding of rational correlations. Marianne swears to her mother that she will never marry unless she can find a man whose taste is fine and matches hers exactly. 'Rapturous delight' (Chapter 4) is the criterion for assessing the truth of taste being expressed. But taste according to Elinor is an 'innate propriety and simplicity', an attribute Edward, she believes, possesses in abundance. When Marianne tentatively questions Edward's taste, Elinor is strong in his defence. He has 'sense and goodness'. His imagination is 'lively, his observation just and correct, and his taste delicate and pure' (Chapter 4, p. 17). For Elinor, matters of taste graduate imperceptibly into matters of judgement. Marianne's understanding of taste is more atavistic, relating more to physical experience and the senses and to the literal interpretation of taste as oral experience, which, Payne Knight reminded his readers, did not derive from the 'higher faculties', but from 'the first that is employed in preserving life by selecting nourishment'.

Taste, we must assume, even in its more general form, is a life preserver. Knight describes taste as 'a general discriminative faculty arising from just feeling and correct judgement implanted in the mind of man by his Creator, and improved by exercise, study and meditation' (19). Taste differs from judgement as wit, which sees resemblances, differs from judgement, which makes comparisons. Judgement is 'the decision, which reason draws from comparison: whence the word is commonly used to signify the talent of deciding justly and accurately in matters, that do not admit of mathematical demonstration, in which sense, judgement may be considered as a mode of action of reason' (236). Reason has 'little or nothing to do with taste; for taste depends upon feeling and sentiment, and not upon demonstration or argument' (236). But, Knight goes on to say, qualifying his case carefully, reason's powers of demonstration are not so powerful as they might seem. This concern with reason leads to considerations which will be explored later. For the moment, it is important to remember that though taste leans toward feeling and judgement to reason, both are founded on moral education and both are *active* faculties which depend on independent judgement. Knight writes as if both are male prerogatives, and in claiming them for her female characters, Jane Austen challenges conventional accounts of what it is appropriate for women to know and how they should conduct themselves.

This becomes clear in a conversation between Elinor, Marianne and Edward, in which Marianne accuses Elinor of conformism because she subordinates her judgement to others. This is manifestly unfair, and Elinor makes the injustice clear:

'But I thought it was right, Elinor,' said Marianne, 'to be guided wholly by the opinion of other people. I thought our judgments were given us merely to be subservient to those of our neighbours. This has always been your doctrine, I am sure.'

'No, Marianne, never. My doctrine has never aimed at the subjection of the understanding . . . You must not confound my meaning. I am guilty, I confess, of having often wished you to treat our acquaintance in general with greater attention; but when have I advised you to adopt their sentiments or conform to their judgment in serious matters?' (Chapter 17, p. 82)

Both women claim independence here, though Elinor goes further and argues that her position is, as Edward terms it, a matter of 'general civility' (p. 82), that is, such conduct conduces to the good order of civic and social life.

Such claims are important. The repressive systems of eighteenth-century conduct books for women refused this independence of thought and the 'opinions' which went with it. 'Girls should be taught to give up opinions betimes, and not pertinaciously carry on a dispute, even if they should know themselves to be in the right . . . they should acquire a submissive temper and a forebearing spirit', wrote Hannah More in her *Essays on Various Subjects, Principally Designed for Young Ladies* (1777).[22] Similar advice was given in 1776 by James Fordyce in his sermon, *The Conduct and Character of the Female Sex*. Likewise, John Gregory spoke of 'that modest reserve, that retiring delicacy' obligatory in women.[23] (Mr Collins, in the later novel *Pride and Prejudice*, chose Fordyce to read to the Bennet girls. Since he is a character manifestly unpleasant, one can safely assume Jane Austen's dislike of these sermons.)

There *is* a difference between the two sisters, but they both believe in independence in a way which means that they take their own aesthetic and moral 'opinions' very seriously indeed. The enquiry going on in the text seems to be less about the validity of having 'opinions' than about the moral and social roots of these convictions. Elinor's aesthetic of the beautiful as useful favours a quieter and less disruptive independence than Marianne, whose individualism, with its preference for 'picturesque' taste rather than 'beautiful' judgement, makes her not so much unaware of propriety but oblivious to the social world. She can contemplate accepting the gift of a horse from Willoughby without seeming to realize the social signals this would give out, or understanding that the expense of an additional servant would be impossible for the Dashwood household. She can transgress convention by looking round a house which belongs neither to her nor to Willoughby and assume that she will come into its ownership. She can be careless and naive. Her reliance on an expressive, psychological intensity untethers her from a social ethic. In that sense she has been read in a derogatory way, as we have seen, as a revolutionary. Certainly her questioning, challenging mind makes for awkwardness. And that there is a politics of the picturesque both inside and outside the novel as a genuine challenge to conformism to which she subscribes is clear. Nevertheless, her feelings do have moral power as well as aesthetic intensity. Her public outburst at the Dashwood dinner in London in defence of Elinor is one of the climactic moments of the novel. She comes into her own, protesting against injustice and coldness. This dissent is scandalous and dreadfully embarrassing to Elinor, but it is surely endorsed in the text. Who could wish the novel to be without this central episode, and who could not feel that this frankness has virtues which the covert, lethal ironies to which Elinor is forced to resort as a mode of defence and dissent cannot possibly possess?

There is a dialectic between taste and judgement in the novel and it is by no means clear that one dominates the other. Both, in Hamlet's words, hold the mirror up to nature and discover something of value. Though the aesthetic argument does give more content to the terms 'sense' and 'sensibility', distributing judgement and taste between them, they are in many ways interdependent rather than antithetical. The aesthetic debate in the novel also gives fuller content to the terminology of connection and attachment. Negative and legal where family and social arrangements are concerned, these terms take on a rather different colour. Elinor favours a world of connection, proportion and rational relationship, beauty as utility, the draftsman's view, perhaps; Marianne favours a less ordered world of discrete sensation, intensity, detail, passionate attachment, a world of interrogation rather than of composure. Whether aesthetic experience is a means of understanding the world and of taking control of their lives as a realistic possibility is one of the dominant preoccupations of the text. In fact what happens is that the intervention of Elinor and Marianne into aesthetic debates problematizes the political and gender implications of the categories of the picturesque. The aesthetic categories they encounter are caught up in power, but the underprivileged Dashwood women do discover modes of self-representation and, through Marianne, critique, even though this means adapting and changing the notion of the aesthetic.

What is clear, however, is that neither of the two sisters, beautiful though they are, conform to the reactionary Burkean standards – highly gendered standards – of the feminized category of the beautiful. Non-rational, passive, small, smooth, delicate in mind and body, affecting the imperfections of weakness and disability, Burke's understanding of the beautiful is repudiated in this text.[24] Possessed of a rich intellectual life, loving vigorous physical exercise, walking in the wind, running, the Dashwood girls have no trace of these debilitating characteristics. Elinor, with her delicate complexion and regular features, perhaps suggests the Burkean paradigm, but her powerful rationality preserves her from it. Marianne, tall in figure, dark-eyed and brown-skinned, exuding the vitality and life which inspires 'delight' (Chapter 10, p. 41), is the antithesis of these conservative values. Her dark beauty aligns her with Price's 'Gipsy' picturesque and not with the conventional European beauty of the white woman. If her energies are disruptive, they are also life-preserving. It is appropriate now to look at her values and the values placed on feeling a little more closely.

Section Three
Women and Men of Feeling

The readings of *Hamlet* which are layered into the novel direct attention towards Marianne. We have seen that the absence of the father figure, the problems of succession and inheritance, and the unsound King, George III, resonate in the novel. Further resonances occur in the use of Uvedale Price's decaying landscape and in the frequent references to Cowper, who sought so strenuously to protect himself, if not from insanity, from profound, depressive instability. Edward's melancholia and lack of confidence, not to speak of indulgent self-pity at times, and his inability to decide what to *do*, are additional registers of a pyschological disability which finds an analogy in *Hamlet*. The war which is not mentioned in the novel appears in this play: the politics of the rotten borough discovers an affinity with the 'rotten' state of Denmark. The oedipal and incestuous alignments between fatherless sons and mother figures, the rivalry between brothers, and the extension of the idea of 'kin' beyond the bound of legitimate definition for the convenience of family aggrandizement, particularly the ambiguous signification of 'cousin' and 'brother', menacingly uncertain words in the play and in the novel, find a context in *Hamlet*. Finally, there is Ophelia, a fatherless girl driven to madness by the murder of her father and the desertion of a lover. One might say that she is driven to madness because she is never really allowed to achieve an identity. Marianne is the analogue here. And in one sense the text is about the impossibility of being Marianne.

It is Marianne's fate to go to the brink of psychological destruction and perhaps beyond. 'Had I died, – it would have been self-destruction' (Chapter 46, p. 293), she says after her recovery, clearly alluding to suicidal feeling. In a moment of extraordinary pathos we are told that the traumatized Marianne is 'unconscious' of the social world and public space, when the sisters are rudely stared at by Robert Ferrars, while shopping in London: 'for she was as well able to collect her thoughts within herself, and be as ignorant of what was passing around her, in Mr Gray's shop, as in her own bedroom' (Chapter 33, p. 187). The slight stumbling of the syntax here betrays, and even participates in, the shocking psychological condition it describes. To be unable to discriminate between public and private space suggests a derangement of an advanced kind. Moreoever, the juxtaposition of commercial shop and bedroom, with its association of exposure, nakedness and sexuality, is a remarkable way of demonstrating Marianne's damaged consciousness. It recalls Ophelia's madness, 'distracted, and with her hair down' (IV v), and fuses a number of moments in the play. Hamlet's invasion of the intimacy of Ophelia's closet (II i), the bedchamber scene with Gertrude (III iv) and the infamous 'Get thee to a nunn'ry' episode (III i) are conflated in this briefest of descriptions. For Marianne, psychologically in her bedroom but actually standing in a commercial place, exposed to the sexual gaze of Robert Ferrars, must be glancingly associated with prostitution. This association is confirmed by John Dashwood a minute or so later when he observes that Marianne's commercial value has depreciated: 'I question whether Marianne *now*, will marry a man worth five or six hundred a-year, at the utmost' (Chapter 33, p. 192). Earlier Marianne herself had been only too aware of the potential prostitution of marriage. She had described a hypothetical union between Colonel Brandon and a suitable older women as little more than a 'commercial exchange' (Chapter 8, p. 33), meaning prostitution. It is an irony that she herself is exposed to the same order of construction later by marrying Brandon. Her proud refusal to consider '"setting one's cap at a man" or "making a conquest"' (Chapter 9, p. 40) in the days before she fell in love with Willoughby contrast with the extraordinary vulnerability to which she is subsequently reduced. Society recognizes feminine sexuality only through the vocabulary of prostitution and commodity.

The narrative later describes the dangerous propensity of events to unsettle Marianne's mind (Chapter 32, p. 179), but the suggestion is also that it takes just the slightest deviance from norms of behaviour for a young woman to be thought of as virtually mad, and sexually uncontrolled as well as mentally uncontrolled. Madness is culturally defined. Marianne's vitality endows her with an actual and potential propensity for volatility, anger and aggression (features of Ophelia's madness, too) which occasion discomfort even before the desertion of Willoughby. We can be driven mad by love and by society's interpretation of our grief as a 'nervous' (Chapter 32, p. 184) complaint, as Elinor defensively – and protectively – describes Marianne's condition to John Dashwood. Elinor constantly attempts to rescue Marianne from public misinterpretation, whether it is the moment of Willoughby's accidental and unutterably cruel meeting with her in London or in John and Fanny Dashwoods' drawing room.

It is generally assumed that it is Marianne's excess of sensibility, and a certain self-indulgent streak, which lead logically to her devastated psychic state. There is a warrant for this ethical and psychological view both in the novel and outside it. Marianne's mourning at the death of her father is excessive, we are told. Her reaction to the departure of Willoughby from Barton is extravagantly melodramatic, as she shuns company and, driven by an unhealthy repetition compulsion, induces grief, and presumably remembered erotic feeling, by returning to the music and songs which they had played together. Elinor is disturbed by such luxuriance, and such a response finds its echo in contemporary accounts of hysteria and medical analyses of excessive feeling. Defining 'Hysterica' (*sic*) in his *A Medicinal Dictionary* (1743), for instance, R. James wrote:

young Women, whose nervous Systems are delicate and weak, who are of a tender Habit, and subject to exorbitant Sallies of lawless Passion, are in greater Danger of this spasmodic Disease, than those who are robust, hardy, laborious, and of a more steady Mind.[1]

The connection of over-intense sensibility with sexuality and its scandal is either overt, as above, or implicit. Mary Wollstonecraft, in her famous *Vindication of the Rights of Woman* (1792) spoke of women's 'over-exercised sensibility', so that 'all their thoughts turn on things calculated to excite emotion and feeling, when they should reason'.[2]

She castigated the restlessness, instability, extremes of feeling (a veering from intensity to boredom) and fitful concentration of the woman whose feelings were indulged without being trained in judgement, a situation which is a 'mixture of madness and folly!' Wollstonecraft's position is endorsed at every point by innumerable conduct books and didactic manuals on feminine behaviour, whether their provenance is conservative or radical.

If not insane, Marianne might be moving towards psychic prostration. After the desertion of Willoughby she moves restlessly from place to place, in a condition of susceptible irritability, scarcely noticing the external world, inattentive, failing to hear or see those around her, indifferent to pleasure or pain, and keeping as far as possible out of the world of social events and activities. Her behaviour follows that described in Richard Payne Knight's critique of the person of sensibility.

In proportion as persons are respectively liable, by the natural constitution of their minds and bodies, to associate their ideas in these several trains, their dispositions are melancholy or gay; and if either be carried to such excess as to break the natural connection, or derange the natural order of them, the effect is lunacy: whence that malady is often partial, affecting some particular trains of ideas, which have been connected with violent or long-continued emotions of affection or passion ... some persons have constitutionally such a vivacity of spirits – such a restlessness rather than fertility of imagination, ever showing itself in new combinations of imagery, sometimes just and pleasing, and some-times the reverse, that they may properly be said to live naturally in a state bordering on intoxication ... for such persons have always their ebbs and flows of spirits; the fit of vivacity being invariably followed by one of the dejection.[3]

Elinor characterizes Marianne as a person of 'animation', but not often 'really merry' to Edward (Chapter 17, p. 82), almost as if endorsing this account of the temperament of sensibility.

Is Marianne's condition presented as a moral cautionary tale? This is one reading, but the text is more generous than to offer a single view of her state. How, then, is she being explored?

Marianne's situation, and the incorporation of 'sensibility' into the title of the novel, might well have seemed slightly old-fashioned by the first decade of the nineteenth century. The cult of sensibility had reached its peak and, since the 1790s, came under increasing criticism from both conservative and radicals alike. A well-known cartoon by James Gillray portrayed a false Sensibility, Rousseau in hand, lamenting the death of a bird while resting a foot on the head of Louis XVI. Radicals, on the other hand, associated sensibility with a refinement which left social problems untouched.[4] The animus of Wollstonecraft's radical attack on sensibility comes from her understanding that to feel was no substitute either for analysis or action. The huge literature of sensibility embodied in the sentimental novel, both by men and women, cannot be an object of detailed discussion here, but it must be empha-sized that by 1811 the dominance of sentimental writing of this kind was on the wane. The literature concerning men of feeling, stemming from Samuel Richardson's *Sir Charles Grandison* (1753–4), which por-trays the life of a good man, balancing his *Clarissa* (1744–8), belongs to the three decades between the 1740s and 1770s. The first volume of Sarah Fielding's *Adventures of David Simple*, for instance, exploring the condition of the man seeking benevolence and affective relationships, was published in 1744. Oliver Goldsmith's *Vicar of Wakefield* (1766), Lawrence Sterne's *Sentimental Journey* (1768) and Henry Mackenzie's *The Man of Feeling* (1771), examples of the genre at its high point, were published considerably before Jane Austen's novel was begun. The novel of the woman of sensibility, often following the pattern of Rousseau's *Julie, ou la Nouvelle Heloise* (1761), as well as adapting the paradigm of *Clarissa*, also belong to a rather earlier phase. Charlotte Brooke's *The History of Lady Julia Mandeville* (1763), Henry Mackenzie's

Julia de Roubigne (1777), Charlotte Smith's *Emmeline* (1788), and Mary Wollstonecraft's *Mary, A Fiction* (1788), either adopt the pattern of a family which forbids the love of the heroine or explore the plight of the wronged woman who is caught up in a legal system and a society beyond her control. Richardson's belief in 'Softness of heart' and 'gentleness of manner' dominates the account of femininity.

But several features distinguish *Sense and Sensibility* from the sentimental literature both of the man and the woman of feeling. To begin with, nothing in Jane Austen's novel exemplifies what one might call the derivative post-Humean moral consensus that benevolence and tenderness are both important and *realizable* virtues. The seeking out of the small nuclear family, either surrogate or biological, in order to confront the world and compensate for social evils, which are seen but not remedied, is not the pattern of Jane Austen's fiction. On the other hand, her novel is just as far from the fiction of the woman of feeling. The central figure of the enforced or wronged woman betrayed by family does not enter *Sense and Sensibility*, and nor does the vocabulary of feminine softness, pliancy and passivity. Indeed, this vocabulary of femininity is implicitly robustly challenged.

Is there nothing in the novel which we might want to relate to the earlier fictions? One novel stands out among man of feeling fiction, a satirical, self-conscious work which has a bizarre relationship with *Sense and Sensibility*, and this is Henry Mackenzie's *The Man of Feeling* (1771).[5] As one considers this text, with its radical pretensions (Mackenzie was concerned with editing the work of Tom Paine, the radical polemicist), it appears to be filling in the unsaid, unmentioned (and unmentionable) experiences of Jane Austen's novel. At the same time she seems to be re-writing Mackenzie's text as her novel proceeds, offering a satire upon a satire. This issues in a new, 'strong' interpretation of 'sensibility', rather than the weak reading of it in novels of sentiment. This is why I have suggested that her novel is a challenge to Jane Austen's culture. Marianne's status is bound up with Mackenzie's text and the way it can be read.

It is as if Jane Austen through her own novel has deliberately created a text which has some of the features of the picturesque scene we associate with Marianne. The movement from location to location, for instance, and the mysterious departures, first of Colonel Brandon and then of Willoughby, create that unease of 'irritable', aroused enquiry and curiosity which is the essence of the picturesque as Price described it. The puzzling, inexplicable behaviour, first of Colonel Brandon, then of Edward at Barton Cottage and finally of Willoughby in London create a discontinuous narrative of gaps and lacunae. It is not a narrative of connection and cohesion despite its fascination with this kind of orderliness; it is much more like a narrative of sharp breaks and intensities, which suggest the aesthetic of 'attachment', the aesthetic of the discrete, intense moment, when the individual detail arouses and intrigues. For the text proceeds as a series of slow-paced events succeeded by climactic moments in which astonishing but frequently incomplete revelations occur. The emotional chiascuro of the novel, its light and shade of waiting and discovery, creates a narrative of extraordinary tension. The high moments of revelation – Lucy's assertion that she is engaged to Edward Ferrars, the return of Marianne's letters by Willoughby, Colonel Brandon's story of a double seduction and prostitution, and Willoughby's confession to Elinor after a race against time across the south of England, are moments of intense emotion, but moments about which even then the novel is reticent. To fill in the gaps, and to think more fully about the social critique being explored, it is necessary to have recourse to Mackenzie's text and to Jane Austen's quizzical relationship to the man and the woman of feeling. The reader is involved in interrogation, of Jane Austen's text, and in addition her reading of Mackenzie. Her text presupposes the active, enquiring reader and a questioning, hermeneutic alertness, exactly the qualities of the critical reader demanded by Price.

Mackenzie's novel shares with Jane Austen's the reference to *Hamlet*. Its protagonist, Harley, another fatherless son whose sole relation is an elderly aunt obsessed with the family name, finds the world a harsh and duplicitous place: it 'Will smile, and smile, and be a villain'. But the main allusion is to a mad woman crossed in love who sings in Bedlam a song adapted from Ophelia's fragmented ballads.

> Light be the earth on Billy's breast,
> And green the sod that wraps his grave.[6]
> (Mackenzie)

> He is dead and gone,
> At his head a grass-green turf,
> At his heels a stone.
> (Shakespeare *Hamlet*, IV V 30–32)

Where Brandon's tale of prostitution hints, Mackenzie's is graphic: where Jane Austen's critique of family and finance is reticent, Mackenzie's is outspoken; where Jane Austen hints of the violence of the colonial imperative in India, Mackenzie is fiercely explicit.

More important still, Mackenzie adopts an extreme form of the picturesque (rather than picaresque) narrative technique intended to arouse and to stimulate hermeneutic and ideological questioning. The narrator's shooting companion has used the manuscript of the novel as wadding for his gun, and so the novel begins in the sixth chapter. There are breaks, lacunae and gaps throughout, so that interpretative emphasis is thrown on the 'remaining' material. Jane Austen fills in the gaps in her novel with another text constructed out of blanks and silences. Thus the urge to interrogate is doubly intensified. Let us consider what Mackenzie's text fills in, what questions have to be asked, and how Jane Austen ironically qualifies *The Man of Feeling*.

Harley and his companions visit Bedlam, and here they discover and view as spectacle and picturesque vignette the girl mad with love. The tragic intensity and extremity of women's sexuality when it has no outlet fills in the gaps in Marianne's history with an intensity and an exposure of grief and display of sexual feeling unknown to the surface text of *Sense and Sensibility*, performing a kind of latent text to Jane Austen's novel, in Freudian terms a 'manifest' text.

The later manifest text figures fragments of the mad woman's discourse: the 'little garnet ring', which fixes her thought is allocated to Edward, the ring noticed but misunderstood by Elinor in Austen's narrative: the motif of the forced marriage to an older man in the Bedlam girl's story, 'Old enough to be her grandfather', surfaces in the manifest narrative in Marianne's dread of a 'second attachment', which will secure her to Colonel Brandon – simultaneously a dread of, possibly, and a desire for, a father figure; the young girl's lover has died and she refuses to marry her father's choice of husband and her 'pale and wasted' face shadows Marianne, who, as John Dashwood remarks, 'has lost her colour, and is grown quite thin' (Chapter 33, p. 192). The conventions of madness are used without stint here, but their very conventionality gives them force:

The unfortunate young lady had till now seemed entranced in thought, with her eyes fixed on a little garnet ring she wore on her finger; ... my Billy is no more! said she, Do you weep for my Billy. Blessings on your tears! I would weep too, but my brain is dry; and it burns, it burns, it burns! – she drew nearer to Harley. – Be comforted, young lady, said he, your Billy is in heaven. – Is he, indeed? and shall we meet again? and shall that frightful man (pointing to the keeper) not be there? – Alas! I am grown naughty of late; I have almost forgotten to think of heaven: yet I pray sometimes; when I can, I pray; and sometimes I sing, – you shall hear me – hush! ... I am a strange girl; – but my heart is harmless: my poor heart; it will burst some day; feel how it beats: – she pressed his hand to her bosom, then holding her head in the attitude of listening – Hark! one, two, three! be quiet thou little trembler? (*The Man of Feeling*, 28–9)

The physical importunateness here and the intense sexual desire suggested by 'it burns' are subliminal presences in Marianne's experience. The story of the abandoned girl is replicated with variation in Mackenzie's second story of betral, the account of the prostitute seduced by Winbrooke. Billy / William / Winbrooke / Willoughby: the resemblances are generic as the culture of the libertine is played out. What is described as Emily's experience enacts what could have happened to Marianne, and what did happen to Eliza and to her daughter, Eliza. Seduction followed by prostitution, followed by rescue is common to Emily in Mackenzie's text and the two Elizas in Jane Austen, who conflates the history of the three women. This story of seduction, euphemistically told, once by Colonel Brandon and once by Willoughby in Jane Austen's text, unfolds explicitly in great detail, told with intensity and passion, just as in the mad woman sequence, by the woman herself, in *The Man of Feeling*. In Mackenzie's text the women speak; they are silent in Jane Austen's text. After Harley visits the scene of squalor and destitution where Emily lives – 'in the darkest corner stood something like a bed, before which a tattered coverlet hung by way of a curtain' – Emily tells her story. It begins as a parallel to Marianne's story, except that the mother is absent, just as in the case of the two Elizas. Emily settles with her father in honourable poverty in a rural village – 'we passed our time in a state of tranquility'. She is an intellectual and free–thinker, who has ignored conventional morality (like the older Eliza), and when Winbrooke comes on to the scene the process of seduction is conducted through the mutual reading and discussion of books:

He would be respectfully attentive all the while, and when I had ended, would raise his eyes from the ground, look at me with a gaze of admiration, and express his applause in the highest strain of encomium ... he asked my opinions of every author, of every sentiment, with that submissive diffidence which showed an unlimited confidence in my understanding. I saw myself revered as a superior being. (*The Man of Feeling*, 49)

The same pattern occurs in the manifest, or surface, text:

Encouraged by this to a further examination of his opinions, she proceeded to question him on the subject of books; her favourite authors were brought forward and dwelt upon with so rapturous a delight, that any young man of five and twenty must have been insensible indeed, not to become an immediate convert to the excellence of such works, however disregarded before. Their taste was strikingly alike. (79)

Neither man seems to have read the books his lady praises. Emily's hubris, pleasure in intellectual power and superiority (rather than mutual delight, as with Marianne) is soon over. Her poverty and economic dependence is exploited. She pursues Winbrooke to London (like Marianne, like young Eliza) believing that he will marry her. He seduces her instead. 'Honour, my Emily, said he, is the word of fools, or of those wiser men who cheat them' (53). Unscrupulously abandoned, starving and ill, she is at the point of death when Harley discovers her. Her father rediscovers her and saves her from further brutalization. 'Villain, he cried' (57). Again, the melodrama sounds out. It is a hackneyed story of 'blasted' sexual honour, but this dreary and brutalizing repetition is exactly the point. The jargon of literary seduction may have pulled away from the social reality of prostitution but prostitution is ever-present as a social reality and as *text* nonetheless. It is partly because Willoughby thinks of his exploitative sexual life as a *style* that he is able to act as carelessly as he does. That masculine freedom is predicated on prostitution is a fact of life. But in Mackenzie's text sexual exploitation is allowed to speak, just as sexual feeling is allowed to speak. The pressure of this undertext on the narratives of Brandon and Willoughby, and the pressure of sexual feeling itself, *feminine* sexual feeling, affords relief to Jane Austen's text, even when the strategies of repression occur.

Through its silences and gaps, Jane Austen's text represents the condition which means that feminine sexual feeling *cannot* find a voice in Marianne's social world. Yet the Mackenzie analogues, conflated and refigured in her text, afford it relief. And some of the undertext, as we may call it, seeps into Austen's manifest narrative. Willoughby reminds Elinor of the young Eliza's importunate desire. That feminine desire should be described by its exploiter is a bitter fact but it does thereby gain expression.

The models and types for John Dashwood and Mrs Ferrars (indeed, all the powerful elderly women of the novel) pre-exist in macabre, inverted form in Mackenzie's text. In Bedlam a mathematician ceaselessly works through calculations on investment in stock, South Sea annuities, India stock, and Three percent annuities consol. He once possessed a great estate of £50,000 a year but has been reduced to poverty and financial failure because his obsession with investment became all consuming. Harley's aunt is another obsessive. For her it is the family name, even to the most distant relatives, which requires perpetuation. But her understanding of family is naive and archaic: she does not understand that in an entrepreneurial culture investment in family and finance should be intertwined; 'but nowadays it is money, not birth, that makes people respected', she says uncomprehendingly (*The Man of Feeling*, 93).

The critique of financial exploitation and outright corruption is at its most intense in the discussion of the British officer in India. Britain's right to trade, says Harley, describing exactly the transformation of Britain's relations with India in the eighteenth century, has been displaced by ruthless financial exploitation, unlawful ownership and the establishment of empire cynically kept in place by a British army which enriches itself unscrupulously as the price of support. Building on Clive's victories and his policy of installing indigenous puppet regimes from which he exacted protection money, the British made colossal fortunes which paradoxically threatened the stability of the East India Company itself.[7] Ruthless individual exploitation and extortions on the part of both servants of the company and soldiers forming the military presence in India occasioned two attempts to control the machinery of government in East India, North's Regulating Act (1773) and Pitt's India Act (1784). Harley's analysis follows the narrations of a 'good' soldier and ex-servant, Edwards, who has returned from India to poverty at home. Here we have the unspoken background to Colonel Brandon's Indian experiences.

You tell me of immense territories subject to the English: I cannot think of their possessions, without being led to enquire, by what right they possess them. They came there as traders, bartering the commodities they brought for others which their purchasers could spare; and however great their profits were, they were then equitable. But what title have the subjects of another kingdom to establish an empire in India? to give laws to a country where the inhabitants received them on the terms of friendly commerce?

When shall I see a commander return from India in the pride of honourable poverty? ... they are covered with the blood of the vanquished! ... did he return with the consciousness of duty discharged to his country, and the humanity of his fellow-creatures; did he return with no lace on his coat, no slaves in his retinue, no chariot at his door, and no burgundy at his table; – these were laurels which princes might envy – which an honest man would not condemn! (*The Man of Feeling*, 88–9)

These passages, on female madness, on prostitution, on finance and family, and above all on India, provide a vociferous, insistent undertext to Jane Austen's novel, an undertext almost unruly, certainly demanding, exposing the unsaid in the surface text. That they present certain stereotypes and moral platitudes in no way detracts from their power. The suffering of women, the brutality of rampant prostitution, the ruthlessness of family strategy and the violence of empire are not diminished by being presented in a slightly stylized form, a kind of eighteenth-century Brechtianism, a technique of alienation and distancing. The raw sexuality of the mad girl, for instance, is contained in the strategies of conventional, Ophelia-like stylization.

But we have said that there are gaps in the undertext, and these make the relation of Mackenzie's novel to Jane Austen's complex. Mackenzie does not simply function as a suppressed underworld. Far from it: it is almost as if Jane Austen's text beckons to his by way of explication of her own. And here is the difficulty, for Mackenzie's text has a problematic relation to Jane Austen's because of its own unsolved questions. It is sometimes said that the novel of sentiment fails to make an adequate political analysis of the social ills it records. This is not quite true in Mackenzie's case. He understands the change of policy and power structure in India, for instance, and his critique of the culture of libertinage is powerful. It is not his analysis but its method of exposing social evils which is a problem. In addition his solutions to social evils are simplistic.

The discontinuous method of narrative, breaking down episodes into discrete, intensely felt descriptions, the picturesque method of arousal and challenge, works against itself. What occurs is not so much the stimulus to make connections but a radical disconnection which prevents them being fully made. There is a tendency for this kind of novel to become a voyeuristic peepshow of separate incidents. One cannot *connect*, for instance, exploitation in India and exploitation of prostitutes. This is compounded by the simple nature of Mackenzie's solutions to the problems he exposes. On many occasions the simplistic response is clearly satirical, an ironic parody of an inadequate affective response to a situation far too serious to warrant trivialization by the feelings. But this is not always so. We can laugh at Harley's tendency to sigh and drop a tear at the sound of the shepherd's horn: his naive goodness, constantly gulled and duped, is also a source of comedy; but more serious is that his solution to social evils is a moralized version of the individualism which has created them. Benevolence is seen as the prerogative of individual acts of kindness. The only solution to lack of benevolence and inhumanity is to retreat to small groups of individuals who can redress these deficiences through a personal reversal of values. If the world at large lacks humanity and benevolence then we must 'strengthen them in ourselves' (90). One prostitute can be rescued, one man can be offered livelihood (Edwards can be given the living he has lost by the gift of a farm), one soldier can be asked to come back poor from India. 'We blame the pride of the rich, said he, but are we not

ashamed of our own poverty?' (93). The failure of individual charity
and its emasculated ethic is perhaps conceded in the death of Harley,
who expires in front of the woman he loves upon learning that she is
still in love with him. Solutions do not arise if you blame yourself for
social evils and not the evils themselves.

How, then, does Mackenzie's text return upon *Sense and Sensibility*?
To begin with, it clarifies some characters and problematizes others
because they are both like and unlike the types of the undertext. While
Marianne's frightful suffering is surely given its full due, her sexual
vulnerability is also emphasized by the parallel, simply because the
condition of the upper-class girl is too *like*, not unlike, the condition of
the prostitute. Even though the gap between Marianne and Emily/Eliza
is socially uncrossable they are all in a situation *structurally* alike.
Marianne's intellectuality, seen as conducive to a sense of power by
Mackenzie, is genuinely enabling in Jane Austen's text, on the other
hand. The problem with it is that it is not powerful enough: as Claudius
says of Ophelia, Marianne's self is 'divided'; she is split between an
aristocratic understanding of hierarchy and ownership, of pre-judged,
fixed positions, and the more radical, mobile questioning and interrogation to be found in her picturesque aesthetic. This splits her morality as
well as splitting her vision.

The great question is whether Marianne capitulates to a materialistic
understanding of marriage when she marries Brandon, whose 'Indian'
background is so clearly described by Mackenzie, and whether this
silences her, denying the values she has so strenuously defended. These
questions change their nature in the context of Willoughby/Winbrooke's
demonstration of sensibility. His great moment, of course, is the
moment of the repentant rake, the moment of breathtaking glamour
and sexual intensity when he arrives at what he believes to be the dying
Marianne's place of rest. The fluency and the passion of his confession,
his self-castigation and remorse, disguise the exactness of his resemblance to Mackenzie's Winbrooke. Even Elinor is taken in by a monstrous piece of self-indulgence. His amnesia about the pathetic Eliza,
who has given birth to his child, has already been mentioned. Perhaps
the most telling moment of the confession, however, is his response to
the news that Marianne is safe from harm and likely to live. 'Had I
known as much half an hour ago – But since I *am* here . . .' (Chapter
44, p. 270). In other words, the thought of Marianne's dead body
prompted his sentimental journey. Willoughby would not have called
on Elinor had he known Marianne to be alive. He would, as he makes
clear, have saved himself the trouble. It was the thought of her romantic

death which urged him to her side in contrition. Marianne alive was a very different matter. The confession emerges because Willoughby's actual arrival in the house urges him to do *something*, and moral posturing is one form of response. But knowing Marianne to be alive, his first response is to ask what Elinor thinks of *him*. 'Do you think me most a knave or a fool?' (p. 270). It is a question which entirely disregards the state of Marianne's mind and feelings. The grossness of this moment is present as moral and psychological critique of individual actions, but it also demonstrates the dialectical relationship of sentimentality and cruelty which dominates not individual actions alone but society at large. *Individual* acts of feeling are the other side of *social* violence. Self-love and social are not the same. Willoughby, Hamlet in the grave of Ophelia, comes to Marianne's 'deathbed' to please himself, and he is able to do so because the culture of libertinage allows him to. His wife, his obligations to his marriage, do not play any part in his decisions at this point. Willoughby is still living as a rake within the institution of marriage because the rake is institutionalized. That is the lesson Mackenzie enables us to hear.

'I loved Ophelia.' Willoughby's confession, if that is what it really is, does however afford Marianne the knowledge, cruelly withheld until this point, that she has been longing for, and for the want of which she has remained ill. A side effect, almost an accident, of his visit is that she is able to know that he loved her in his way. The appalling 'agony' (Jane Austen's word) of rejection and its meaninglessness is assuaged. Marianne is ready to get better because she no longer has to experience the treadmill of repetition in Bedlam, the endless mourning process of blocked grief, which comes about because her situation cannot be given any explanation. Willoughby redeems her without knowing it and without even trying to. It is, perhaps, his loss as well as her gain. Unfinished mourning would have been Marianne's lot without the saving explanation which brings the repeated hermeneutic process of grief, the anxious questioning of the bereaved lover, to an end. And here one of the great insights of the novel emerges. One might see Marianne's mourning process, essentially the symptom of blocked questions, very much as a negative form of picturesque arousal. The eager curiosity and critical interrogation summoned by the experience of the picturesque is analogous to the darker interrogations of melancholia. It is entirely appropriate that Marianne should move from one to the other. And the aesthetic condition of hermeneutic arousal and the lonely questioning of bereavement share an important characteristic. They occur alone. Neither the picturesque nor the solipsism of melancholy presuppose the presence of the mind of another as part of the questioning process. Marianne gets better when somebody else helps her to answer her questions and enables her to make an analysis of her situation, a process continued with the help of Elinor.

Thus the hermeneutic challenge which is one form of sensibility is empowered when it is shared, when it is genuinely social and when knowledge becomes a matter of shared enquiry and not power. It is characteristic of Jane Austen's work that this insight comes about in the context of sexual relations; most of her insights do. One way of looking at this is to see the incipient political questions being invoked here as safely subsumed in the domestic and sexual space. This would give us the conservative reading of Jane Austen which is often available in her work. The sexual politics of love as a shared project is a harmonious resolution of Marianne's dilemma. But however attractive, this misses the intellectual element which is so insistently present throughout the novel, and falls back into an affective sensibility which seems to be being systematically rejected by the text.

Another way of reading the elision of the arousals of the picturesque and the interrogations of melancholy is to see the political and social importance of the model of sexual power relationships and the epistemology of the lover's discourse. Heterosexual love is the central relation of many women's lives in Jane Austen's novels and to be liberated at one blow from the naked individualism of sexual relations into the social relations of shared knowledge and enquiry is an extraordinary act of emancipation. The move is from power relations and lonely enquiry, or individual enquiry which bears all the marks of hermeneutic violence, to a collective enquiry which is genuinely political because it is not solitary. 'Your Billy is in heaven,' Harley assures the grieving woman in Bedlam, with all the superficiality of affective sensibility. 'Is he indeed?' is the sceptical and canny answer. The sentimental explanation won't do. But the explanation with analytical possibilities will help. However inadvertently, Willoughby provides these possibilities as he shares in Marianne's explanatory project. For Marianne does not simply discover that Willoughby loved her: she knows that he did not love her enough to marry her; the work she has to do on her experience is analytical, not sentimental. But all the qualifications we make around the moment of Marianne's release, it holds out a flickering emancipatory possibility, a transformation of sexual relations, power and knowledge through participatory enquiry.

What of Colonel Brandon, who has come back from India, it seems, not with lace on his collar but requiring those unerotic flannel waistcoats, possibly induced by a malarial condition? By critics generally he is not looked kindly upon as Marianne's husband. He represses and controls her sexuality by muting her vivacity. She may even have married him for money. These are some of the disappointed conclusions elicited by the match. Jane Austen's comedy never quite allows the satisfaction of the dreamwork's desires. A moral Willoughby, after all, is a contradiction in terms.

Let us consider Brandon. He was with his regiment for three years in India after the disaster of his disappointment over Eliza. He seems to have made enough money, so Mrs Jennings has discovered, to pay off the debts on the Delaford estate and is reckoned to be rich. He was quite certainly involved in the system of colonial exploitation in India: he may even have the blood of the slaughtered on his hands. Harley believes all those who return from India can hardly help being stained by it. There is no evidence that Colonel Brandon, a younger son who has profited from it in typical eighteenth-century fashion, resists colonial ideology. He is modest, however, in his expenditure, rejecting the gold lace, the imported slaves and the burgundy. He is well enough off to give the Delaford living to Edward. If he had had pretensions to great power and influence through wealth he would not, we assume, have come to be a friend of the not very important Middletons. When first seen he is slightly uneasy with them in any case, as if he is finding it difficult to get used to the pleasure principle again after the return from India and the discovery of the destitution of Eliza, even though these events occurred fourteen years ago, not long after the time Marianne was born. He hints at them to Elinor as if they were recent occurrences (Chapter 11). He does not hunt, so far as we can see, and neither does he dance – or sing. There is something inhibited about him to be sure.

But he is a sensitive man as well as being the man of sense Elinor finds him to be. He defends Marianne and her dogmatism about the second attachment against Elinor's extremely rigorous strictures. The 'romantic refinements of a young mind' should not be forced to give way to more 'dangerous' opinions, that is, to cynicism and careless disregard of self in sexual matters (Chapter 11, p. 50). Deeply held feeling, for himself as her first love, we assume, might have rescued the desperate Eliza from the adultery – for her this turned out to be a form of prostitution rather than sexual pleasure – to which she turned to escape from his loveless brother. He adopts in some ways the ethic of *The Man of Feeling*, where we are reminded that, 'our boys are prudent too soon' (71). But Marianne is not sentimentalized by him – rather taken a little over seriously. It is hard to know how to respond to his view of her. In some ways to grant her the right of her romanticism is to grant her autonomy. It may also be that romantic feeling as against false notions of sexual freedom, which he implicitly attributes to Eliza, is seen as the lesser of two evils. Or it may be that he thinks of both women in terms of the need to control their sexual energy. Though he watches the dancing Marianne with physical pleasure, and rescues the sick and dying Eliza when the situation has got well beyond the relevance of sexual control. He is conventional, perhaps, about sexual virtue, but goes to the furthest point of middle-class liberalism by making strenuous efforts to rescue both Elizas. He is, perhaps, neither particularly advanced nor particularly reactionary as far as both sexual and political mores are concerned. And this is the point. He is about as decent a man as could be, given the crushing pressures on men not to be decent. And that is saying something.[8]

And there are other, more lovable and quixotic characteristics. He once thought of eloping, and would have done but for discovery. The text suggests no disapproval here. He is prepared to fight a duel, *not* for a relation, or even a distant relation, but for the sake of the child of the woman he first loved and Willoughby's daughter. It is just possible that Harley's 'we are all relations' has something more than sentimental or prudential force in his case. In fact, Colonel Brandon is himself a romantic, a man of sensibility. That he belongs to the category of the new 'strong' man of feeling or sensibility is suggested by his ability to help, sensitively and unconditionally, with knowledge and information at a crucial point in the narrative. The model of social relations with which he works is participatory. He comes forward with information about Willoughby's seduction of his ward after considerable, principled, self-scrutiny, as a way of assisting the explanatory process after Willoughby's desertion of Marianne. There is no element of self-interest, no false sentiment. There is nothing he can gain from this action. That there is a principled romantic beneath the flannel waistcoat becomes clear in the text, and surely clear to Marianne, who has the satisfaction of marrying a father figure as well as a man of sensibility.

At over thirty-five years of age and after a period of sexual restraint, Colonel Brandon marries Marianne. This may seem to many a low-toned culmination. But it is nevertheless a union of two kinds of romantic, two people of sensibility, one questioning and interrogative (Marianne), one compassionate and feeling (Brandon). If Brandon seems inhibited at times, isn't this because he is sensitive? The match seems surprising and even dull, but the union does not put sense and sensibility in antithesis to one another, for Colonel Brandon is capable of taking rash and passionate action on several occasions. Both a man and a woman of feeling come together in the match.

Does the union suggest the text's careful and qualified consent to the psychological, aesthetic and political implications of the cult of feeling and sensibility, allowing these to both men and women? Not wholly. The project of the novel appears to be to redefine sensibility, and to shift its meaning from the psychological to the social. True to its roots in sensation, sensibility *is* the arousal of emotion, but the arousal of emotion is a precondition for enquiry and action. The experience of emotion is bound up with an alertness to the problematical, an arousal of the faculties induced by incompleteness. We return to Johnson's association of sensibility with 'quickness', or vitality. Ideally, shared interpretative activity engages with the problematical. This is what saves taste from being merely individual sensation, however refined. Taste becomes a social matter when it involves not just shared experience but shared activity. The difference between *Sense and Sensibility* and a novel such as *The Man of Feeling* is the difference between a model of mind and society which exist apart from one another and an understanding of mind and society in terms of an interactive, challenging relation between institutions and groups. The independent vignettes of individual suffering in *The Man of Feeling* – the mad girls, the prostitute, the old soldier whose son is press-ganged – *are* arousing. Questioning and compassion are the reactions they elicit. They provoke questions which move from the particular to the general: why has this happened? does the single instance exemplify a universal problem? what social arrangements give rise to this suffering? how common is it in society at large? Questioning and compassion are the basis of empathy, or that sympathy valued so highly by those eighteenth-century ethical thinkers writing in the tradition of Shaftesbury. But for Jane Austen's text empathy alone is not a civic virtue. Mackenzie's Harley is prepared to ask and answer questions in isolation. Jane Austen, on the other hand, suggests that these questions cannot be asked and answered alone. Moreover, they cannot be tackled by the implicit quietism which brings about Harley's death. He allows himself to be overwhelmed by emotion which does not issue in action or in thought.

It is hard if not impossible to bring about change, but the right of analysis and critique, the right of satire, remains. The Dashwood girls, remember, are thought of as satirists. Perhaps nothing is more confirming and invigorating as a genuinely social moment than the occasion when Elinor, Marianne and Mrs Jennings 'all joined in a very spirited critique' of John Dashwood's callous response to the misfortunes of Edward (Chapter 37, p. 227). It is Marianne whose indignation 'burst forth' (p. 227): Marianne is repeatedly satirized in the novel for not seeing that an isolationist sensibility is self-destructive as well as socially limiting, but her vivacity, her questioning spirit and her delight in enquiry is endorsed. And when she becomes a *social* being her sensibility is ratified. Her stricken awareness of the pain inflicted on her family by her grief at the end of the novel is, like everything she does, overstated, as excessive as her zealous programme of self-education. But there is a new understanding here, despite the urge to self-punishment. Presumably Colonel Brandon rescues her from this ascetic life. Disappointed readers might give him that credit. The truth is, Willoughby's sexual intensity and charm compel even the most critical readers to relinquish their judgement. Colonel Brandon is not portrayed as an unsexual man. Experience might persuade Marianne to prefer his sensitivity to Willoughby's glamour.

Sensibility, perhaps, seems the most problematic of the two abstract nouns of Jane Austen's title. It bears a huge cultural load, and is difficult to map as a moral, social and political category because there were differing interpretations of its meaning and different and changing evaluations of it over the period Jane Austen was writing her novel. As I have said, conservative and radical critiques of the discourse of sensibility coexisted. However much one tries to clarify it, the meaning of sensibility is volatile in Jane Austen's text and difficult to control because the qualities it denotes are volatile. She herself seems to have trouble controlling its meaning. The text seems to be searching for understanding rather than legislating about sensibility. The novel imagines a world with too much sensibility in Mrs Dashwood, and too little in the other Mrs Dashwood, Fanny. Mrs Dashwood is over-emotional, but Fanny's hysteria on discovering the 'betrayal' of Lucy is the emotion of the woman who is not used to feeling anything. To be ill-educated in the feelings is as troubling as over-educated feelings appear to be. Throughout, the text searches for the meaning of a responsible sensibility capable of being experienced by men and women and compatible with civic virtue.

But the meaning of sense is not self-evident either. It is easy to read the novel as if the category of sense is the simple ground on which we found its opposite, sensibility. But in many ways it is a quality as unstable as that of sensibility. It is time to turn from Marianne, Willoughby and Brandon to Elinor and Edward and the concerns which cluster round them, to see how sense is being explored in the novel.

Section Four
Knowing and Spying: Making the Right Connections – Again

The thematics of *Hamlet* have further resonances in *Sense and Sensibility* when we come to consider the last major concern of the novel, its enquiry into sense and judgement. How is it possible to know, and to know in particular about other people, and what are the permissible limits of such knowledge? How do matters of judgement belong to ethics and to politics, and when does the need to know become the compulsion to spy? The enquiry is both social and epistemological. It will be necessary to say something about different understandings of knowledge and ethics in the eighteenth century. These may seem a little remote from *Hamlet*, so it is appropriate at this point to recapitulate the fleeting and subtle network of *Hamlet* allusions, providing a latent dreamwork text which repeatedly intrudes into the manifest narrative, to suggest how the play is invoked once again to deepen and problematize the text.

The dead or absent father is the first noticeably overdetermined aspect of the novel, two such deaths occurring in the first pages. An experiment with a society from which the father has been subtracted follows from this: fatherless sons and their oedipal impulses, husbandless wives, and fatherless daughters, are multiplied. Analogues in the play, the rivalry of brothers in sexual and heirship struggles, and the incestuous or ambiguous position of the widow in relation to young men, hint of faultlines in the heirarchy of family. It is Claudius, however, confusing the issue by addressing Hamlet by the word son *and* the euphemisms of cousin and brother, whose vocabulary dominates the novel. This fictive language of relationship, invented to preserve a corrupt liaison, is the occasion of Jane Austen's sceptical exploration of family ties, which, the novel shows, were often invented or severed for financial convenience. Consequently the limit case of both the near and the distant relation becomes important. Eighteenth-century ethnography considered the evolution of races and the development of the nation state on the model of a progressively bifurcated family tree.[1] Implicitly the novel tests out this hypothesis through the shadowy presence of Hamlet's 'A little less than kin and more than kind'. One of the most awkward questions of the novel is how we are to think of those who are *not* co-opted into this universal family. This is particularly important because the family is associated with demarcations of class and gender in which people stop 'belonging', like the two Elizas, who, if not prostitutes are fallen women.

The influence of family connection in the rotten borough converges with the 'rotten' state of Denmark. Again, the concealed text does the work of critique. Similarly, the invocation of war in *Hamlet* creates an unsaid context for the novel composed and rewritten through the draining French wars. Marianne's distraction at the desertion of Willoughby, threaded through Hamlet's references to Ophelia's prostitution and the Ophelia-like mad woman and prostitute figures of *The Man of Feeling*, another undertext, hints at the unmentionable nature of intense sexual feeling in women, which is constructed as madness. Willoughby's necrophilia, akin to Hamlet's fascination with Ophelia's grave, is another incidence of the incipient morbidity of Jane Austen's text: 'I had seen Marianne's sweet face as white as death . . . Yet when I thought of her to-day as really dying, it was a kind of comfort to me to imagine that I knew exactly how she would appear to those, who saw her last in this world' (Chapter 44, p. 277). Typically, this is the emotion of the picturesque voyeur. He is thinking of himself, not of Marianne.

The exploration of aesthetic matters, taste and the picturesque is less allusive. Except that *Hamlet* is a play very concerned with aesthetic problems, there are fewer hints of the latent Shakespeare text. A lesser writer might have been more systematic in these concealed, cobweb connections and references. Jane Austen's novel confidently sorts and sifts what it needs and leaves aside what it does not need. For instance, it does not trouble to provide itself with a play within the 'play' of the text. It is, however, during the course of the debate on the picturesque that one comes across some further sinister associative ties with a 'rotten' Hanoverian state. Furthermore, the questions raised by the picturesque involve the problem of *viewing*. Gilpin's aristocratic picturesque of the overview, with its commanding *en face* reading of landscape from a fixed point, is implicitly abandoned in favour of the hermeneutic complexities of bourgeois picturesque reading or viewing of landscape. This form of viewing, we remember, is in terms of the discrete instant, the discontinuous detail: the eye does not grasp a visual field as a whole but through its parts; the result is to foreground the act of interpretation, so that the aroused, active gaze questions and interrogates, synthesizes and reconstructs the visual data before it, travelling across light and shade, considering separate categories of experience. This is the picturesque of Uvedale Price.

There are, however, some connections between references to art and to *seeing* in *Hamlet* and the novel. There appears to be a 'good' picturesque and a 'bad' picturesque, a legitimate and illegitimate form of viewing. The 'good' picturesque arouses the enquiring eye which eagerly questions and constructs relationships. The aesthetic can be transposed to the political and ethical here, as an aroused, interrogative curiosity refuses passivity and claims independence. On the other hand, the 'bad' picturesque fragments experience into the intense, discrete detail experienced for its own sake and for the sake of the intense moment of arousal. This experience is akin to the erotic experience of the voyeur, as the self-contained vignette or striking detail is savoured irresponsibly, detached from or not transmuted to the epistemological impulse. This is taste as voluptuary experience, close to the primal physical experience of the desire for food, as Payne Knight remarked, but now thriving on the uncovering of the scene of visual pleasure. The picturesque can enact the erotics of concealing and revealing. And the vantage from which it is seen resembles the visual privilege of the peepshow, in which the viewer is unseen by the object, or not comprehended by it. Such a case might be the mad woman in Bedlam. This voyeuristic position is not unlike a view from behind the arras. It occurs when the desire to know turns into the desire to spy.

The 'good' and 'bad' picturesque are not easy to distinguish. One can slide into the other. In just the same way the arousal of eager, interrogative curiosity can slide into a greedier epistemephilia, or the will to knowledge driven by an insatiable unconscious. Moreover, when the psychological implications of these desires are seen in terms of social and political relations, what constitutes legitimate knowledge, or what justifies spying, becomes contentious indeed. And this is unalterably, unequivocally, a two-sided, social problem. Once we leave landscape and consider a person or persons as the object of the desire for knowledge, the aesthetic becomes the political. The ethics of enquiry and the rights of the object of enquiry are bound up together. We are suddenly in the terrain of *Hamlet* again. Polonius behind the arras, and Rosencrantz and Guildenstern, are not far away from *Sense and Sensibility*. Mrs Jennings plays Polonius, Lucy and her elder sister play Rosencrantz and Guildenstern.

These are the extreme cases, of course, but this is a novel in which everyone watches each other for good and bad reasons. Delicacy, taste, and sensibility dictate a refusal of unwonted intrusiveness into the privacy of individuals: thus what cannot be directly spoken of has to be tactfully deduced. The polite constraints of taste actually *breed* the intrusion they disavow. But gossip, curiosity and spite can also lead to exactly the same kind of deductive gaze on everyone. And the rigours of a directly *repressive* society create spies. Repression breeds the surveillance of the social spy, and legitimates the political spy. 'By indirections find directions out' (*Hamlet*, II i 66) is the motto of everyone in the novel except, perhaps, Marianne, whether they like it or not. And this situation moves from broad comedy to extreme ethical difficulties of conscience. And by the same token there are comic variants on the 'purposes mistook' (V ii 338), which end *Hamlet*, and subtle problems of perception and misprision.

Before exploring the questions of knowledge and spying, which arise in the novel, it is as well to remember that Jane Austen was living in a war society where surveillance and government spies were the norm. I have mentioned the repressive measures Pitt's government took to quell dissent and Jacobinism. By the time the novel was published he was dead (1806) but repressive measures against sedition, narrowly defined, continued. It was the age of the treason trial: the prosecutions of 1794 culminated in the trial of William Hone in 1817. It was also the age of intense state secrecy and the suppression of information and debate. Stamp duty on newspapers, the tax on knowledge, as it was called, was progressively increased throughout this period and was not reduced until the 1830s. Those who dared to perpetuate the unstamped radical press ran constant risk and frequently incurred imprisonment. Free access to ideas, particularly for the dangerously seditious poorer classes, was deliberately blocked.[2] The brooding, paranoid atmosphere of *Hamlet* is an appropriate analogue for this experience, but in the novel it is transmuted into grotesque comedy. It is as if the painful experience is displaced into burlesque and inverted. For the spiral of secrecy, censorship and surveillance is outrageously open and scandalously on display, an open secret of which people are curiously oblivious. Mrs Jennings is its raucous representative, with her perpetual discoveries, through the semiotics of the blush or look as indicator, of hidden attachments, romance and sexual fancies. Her conversation is one long sexual revelation, one long consent to social spying.

Her major preoccupation, and here another key word of the novel appears, is with the 'match'. It is a crude operation at one level – forcing people together – and she goes through as many variations and combinations as possible, Brandon and her daughter, Marianne and Brandon, Elinor and Brandon. Her cheerful prurience aligns her with

Polonius, for whom sexual attachment is the single, dominant explanation for all behaviour. But at another level the idea of the match epitomizes what everyone in the novel has to do: they make inferences by correlating words and actions. Another preoccupation of *Hamlet*, the gap between words and actions, begins to make itself apparent. 'Suit the action to the word, the word to the action,' Hamlet famously advises the players (III ii 17). Mrs Jennings assertively closes the gap between action and word with her robust sexual literalism – evidence of sexual attraction between two people equals marriage, the ultimate tie in which words are suited to actions in the performative ritual of the marriage service. Hence all the Dashwood circle when in London are assured by acquaintance that Marianne is to marry Willoughby, because Mrs Jennings's gossip has foreclosed on the gap between actions and words. And to discover this relationship – one might say, to force it to come true – Mrs Jennings goes to great lengths, illegitimate lengths, of espionage: she finds informers. 'I know where you spent the morning,' she says to Willoughby and Marianne, using the open secret of the innuendo, when she has discovered about the unwise visit to Allenham (Chapter 13, p. 60). The exchange is worth quoting in full because her unscrupulous methods, both of information gathering and revelation, are disclosed:

Marianne coloured, and replied very hastily, 'Where, pray?'—

'Did you not know,' said Willoughby, 'that we had been out in my curricle?'

'Yes, yes, Mr Impudence, I know that very well, and I was determined to find out *where* you had been to. – I hope you like your house, Miss Marianne. It is a very large one I know, and when I come to see you, I hope you will have new-furnished it, for it wanted it very much, when I was there six years ago.'

Marianne turned away in great confusion. Mrs Jennings laughed heartily; and Elinor found that in her resolution to know where they had been, she had actually made her own woman enquire of Mr Willoughby's groom, and that she had by that method been informed that they had gone to Allenham, and spent a considerable time there in walking about the garden and going all over the house.

The carefully timed revelation of inside knowledge exacts the maximum embarrassment, as does the inference of Marianne's future occupation of Allenham. Mrs Jennings has prior knowledge of the house as well as knowing about the visit of the two young people, and she has used two servants to discover what she wants to know. There is a violence about this episode, a seeking for power, which goes beyond the good-natured joke. It is a libidinal desire for vicarious sexual experience which brings another disturbing note into the novel. I do not mean to suggest that

Mrs Jennings is literally intended to be seen as a government agent rooting out Jacobin sedition. But Jane Austen lived through probably one of the most repressive political eras of recent history, and her texts understand the culture of espionage. The manipulation of servants is not without its significance, raising the problem of class privilege and power relationships as it does by seeing servants in terms of pure instrumentality. The novel describes a world which is not open, but more important than this Mrs Jennings is part of, caught up in, a chronic *structure* of surveillance and concealment. Surveillance breeds concealment and concealment breeds surveillance: secrets breed gossip and gossip breeds secrecy; there is a presupposition that everyone has something to hide, whether in the domestic context or at large in the state. The informer society knows no boundaries.

Mrs Jennings is not the only spy and gossip – the two things are dialectically related – in the novel. John Dashwood and the Steeles share this trait. And they are lesser people because Mrs Jennings's voracious desire to know everything about people is the other side of an intermittent but genuinely human generosity. It is characteristic of this text that the test case for the ethics of spying turns on the erotics of spying in the context of sexual experience, for, as so often in this novel, sexuality through its intensity exposes the extremity of a problem. Translated into the political and ethical sphere, the problem of knowing and the betrayal of spying discloses real social complexities which are intensified through their connection with the libidinal energies released by Mrs Jennings. Before approaching these subtler problems, a glance at the Steeles and their place in the spy network is appropriate.

The comedy of Anne Steele arises from her inability to see what information belongs to the private and the public sphere. Spying at the door upon the occasion of her sister's momentous interview with the penniless Edward, justifying the act with a childhood memory of Lucy eavesdropping by 'hiding in a closet' (Chapter 38, p. 232), moving on intrusively to Elinor's 'spotted muslin' (p. 233), and muddling up the ethics of Lucy's position with the problem of trimming a hat with pink ribbons, she has no sense of social or personal boundaries. 'Get it all out of her, my dear,' Mrs Jennings advises Elinor when Anne is sighted in Kensington Gardens, 'she will tell you anything if you ask' (p. 229). It takes a spy to know a spy. The consequence of Anne's lack of discrimination is that the classification of what really does belong to the private sphere and what to the public is open to question. If everything becomes the object of curiosity no boundaries can exist. When Marianne is still devastated after the revelation of Willoughby's infidelity, the Steeles are prepared to invade her bedroom in order to see her.

It is Lucy, of course, who is the prime spy of real sophistication. Elinor becomes uneasily aware of Lucy's inquisitiveness, and when the revelation of Lucy's engagement to Edward is made, and the news that the hair in Edward's ring is not Elinor's but Lucy's consolidates this information the two women are drawn into a relation of mutal watching, fettered to one another by the need to watch and control each other's knowledge. Lucy's curiosity elicits Elinor's. Lucy, 'her little sharp eyes full of meaning', tries to discover Elinor's feelings for Edward with fake openness: 'I felt sure that you was angry with me' (Chapter 24, p. 123). Elinor, on the other hand, tries to discover the facts and legitimacy of Lucy's relation with Edward with fake politeness: 'Your case is a very unfortunate one; you seem to me to be surrounded with difficulties, and you will have need of all your mutual affection to support you under them' (p. 123). The two women become dependent upon one another for information, and locked into a destructive cycle of detection. The comedy, unusually stylized and formal for Jane Austen, does not detract from the viciousness of the situation, one woman monitoring the other's sexual feeling, the other woman probing the first woman's veracity. Elinor manoeuvres a discussion with Lucy by joining her work for Lady Middleton on the horrid little Annamaria's basket:

Lucy made room for her with ready attention, and the two fair rivals were thus seated side by side at the same table, and with the utmost harmony engaged in forwarding the same work. (Chapter 23, p. 122)

By 'forwarding the same work' the women are not so much concentrating on filligree as mutually furthering surveillance under the guise of confidences. The 'work' is the labour of spying, not sewing. This is a difficult moment for the narrative, because a sharply satirized persona is placed side by side with a character whose interiority has been witnessed throughout the novel. Yet the harshness with which Lucy is treated is a little easier to understand in this context. Like all good spies Lucy is an expert infiltrator, unscrupulously currying favour with Lady Middleton and Fanny Dashwood by displaying false sentiment. In Kensington Gardens Anne speaks of some 'genteel' friends, and it is as much the affectation of gentility as the production of sentiment which makes Lucy so irritating. Her spying project is mounted partly as an act of mimicry, in order that she can enter the upper classes and become one of them. But this mimicry apes the worst characteristics of the upper classes, their heartlessness, their self-promotion, and not their best – though in the terms of this novel it is difficult to find an aristocrat with any good qualities.

It is hard not to feel that in naming the Steeles after a famous literary figure, Jane Austen must have had some motive. Richard Steele, famous essayist and spokesman for a new kind of literary journalism and the values of a middle-class gentility, was preoccupied with the distinction between inherited title and bourgeois merit, and with the veneration and respect due to both. He returned to this theme in well-known articles in *The Tatler* and in his own plays. He was often confused and ambivalent, believing that the rising mercantile classes could make claims for gentility and the softness of sensibility, entering the elite through a 'natural' aristocracy, which preserved the concept of aristocratic privilege while opening the way for bourgeois encroachment on privilege.[3] The middle-class claim to equal aristocratic standing was based on the demonstrable refinement of manners and the visible characteristics of sensibility: style (Steele) rather than ethics thus become paramount, and sensibility a kind of performance of refinement. Affect and *affectation* become closely allied.

If Lucy Steele carries this cultural and class connotation into the novel, the hostility with which she is portrayed perhaps becomes more understandable. However, the Steeles, as I have pointed out, are a node of difficulty in this text, presented with real ambivalence. Satirized for their imitation gentility and sensibility on the one hand, and celebrated subversively for their scandalous ambition on the other, they are a constant irritant in a text which does not know quite what to do with them, however brilliant the rendering of their grotesque false refinement may be. Both sisters, each actually very different from the other, become moving at times, even when there is clearly a will to satire on the part of the text, and both become thinly realized social climbers at others. There is a sneaking doubt at the heart of the text: the future may be on the side of the mimetic social spy. Indeed, perhaps that is what social cohesion means – advance by imitation.

The Steeles open up a major problem for the text and force a confrontation with it: is all knowledge a variant on, a refined form, of spying? The true basis of judgement, Payne Knight said, is comparison.[4] Elinor's experience is at stake here, since she is the representative of rational judgement in the text. Comparison must depend upon scrutiny, investigative scrupulousness, attentiveness, and the ability to match actions and words and assess their meaning. Elinor is constantly confronted with such tasks. At nineteen, we are told, she is gifted with greater powers of discrimination and judgement than her mother, and throughout the novel it falls to her lot to take action and make decisions on the basis of rational assessment. She is in a state of perpetual social alertness. The eager hermeneutic questioning and interrogation characteristic of Marianne is not hers. Elinor is a social watcher. In fact, her *sense* is constantly tested. What does this require of her?

A social alertness almost to the point of tension is required of Elinor. She is hypersensitive to awkward moments on social occasions and deftly deflects difficulties. A typical case is the comedy of the occasion of her joint sewing task with Lucy. In order to manouevre a chance to speak to Lucy she has to find a way of making a polite exit from Lady Middleton's rubber of Casino and of joining Lucy at filligree without dishonestly avowing affection for the 'spoilt child' (Chapter 23, p. 121), an assertion Lucy has no compunction whatever in making, for whom they are sewing. At the same time she has to cover Marianne's carelessness in causing offence to Lady Middleton with the implied criticism of 'I detest cards' (Chapter 23, p. 121) and her flight to the pianoforte. Resourceful praise of the tone of Lady Middleton's pianoforte puts the situation more or less right. The multiple awareness – and strain – required of such social skill is demonstrated in the context of trivial incidents. These indicate the constant responsiveness which is required for the techniques of genteel behaviour in polite society. But the same subtlety and quickness is required for the solution of larger ethical problems.

Several major interpretative tasks which test judgement to the utmost fall to Elinor. They concern herself and other people. All these judgements, even those of the most delicate moral concerns, require 'indirection', a devious means of understanding. In this novel 'indirection' is not so much a moral matter as an epistemological and social fact. The first major problem of judgement is over Marianne's possible engagement to Willoughby. Mrs Dashwood is certain that Marianne and Willoughby have become privately engaged. Elinor believes that there is no evidence for this. Willoughby's mysteriously sudden departure from Allenham provokes these speculations. Mrs Dashwood argues that the couple *behave* as if engaged, and thus appearances permit this deduction. Elinor insists on other kinds of evidence: '"I want no proof of their affection," said Elinor; "but of their engagement I do."' (Chapter 15, p. 70). When Elinor reminds her mother that 'not a syllable' has been spoken of an engagement, she replies: '"I have not wanted syllables where actions have spoken so plainly"' (p. 70). Actions and words do not correlate here, or, at least, there is a profound difference of opinion about them. Thus the ethics of concealment and the ethics of *guessing* become problematical. 'Secrecy may be advisable' (p. 69), Elinor wonders, but cannot see why, believing that concealment is wrong and that only wild speculation can occur without solid proof of the engagement. '*I* require no such proof' (p. 70), her mother asserts. Another result of this ambiguity is that what constitutes empirical evidence also becomes problematical.

The problem is not simply that a formal engagement would permit behaviour that would be deemed impermissible without one: it is not simply a case of conduct; as Marianne becomes increasingly anxious and distressed, Elinor believes that a clarification of the ambiguity of the situation would enable them to help her. Her point is that without knowing, no one knows how to act. Mrs Dashwood, over-concerned with a delicate reserve about intruding on Marianne's privacy, refuses to ask her. With exaggerated respect for the interiority of romantic subjectivity, she reacts with moral horror at the rational suggestion that Marianne – and we remember that she is hardly more than sixteen – should be asked about the truth of the matter. The result of this ambiguity is to force everyone to act indirectly. The built-in deviousness of polite sensibility is made apparent. Elinor wants to cut through it but cannot, because her mother's authority is paramount. No one knows if there is anything to conceal or not.

Elinor's judgement turns out to be right in the case of the 'engagement' of Marianne and Willoughby. With neat symmetry, her assessment of Edward and the puzzle of his relation to Lucy, turns on exactly the opposite conditions. Lucy's engagement to him is supported by 'a body of evidence'. Lucy offers her a picture, a letter, and an explanation for the hair in Edward's ring. With this knowledge Elinor goes on to deduce the psychological circumstances of the situation: 'Had he feigned a regard for her which he did not feel? Was his engagement to Lucy, an engagement of the heart? No . . .' (Chapter 23, p. 117). But she then goes on to assure herself of 'the necessity of concealing' her non-engagement to Edward from her mother and Marianne, ending up in the same position as her sister though for different reasons. She must not grieve her mother and sister. Also, 'She was stronger alone', a fusion of narrative voice and an internal monologue avows (p. 119). So both sisters end up concealing a non-engagement, but one, Elinor, deals in evidence, while the other, Marianne, never considers it.

This artful symmetry between the two sisters is, of course, a constant resource of the narrative. The relation between them calls forth the act of comparison, the act on which the faculty of judgement is founded, or so some eighteenth-century thinking would have it. The text is organized so that its own structure makes this comparative act necessary (and even the act of spying) on the reader's part. Perhaps this is another reason for the intensive doubling of figures and experiences in the novel – to provide comparative instances. This means that Elinor, the judge, the watcher, the figure to whose consciousness we are nearest, because it is nearest to, and often converges with, the narrative voice, herself becomes the object of judgement. From the very beginning we are told of Elinor's superior judgement and of her capacity to 'govern' (p. 6) her feelings. The firmness of the statement deflects criticism from her, but does the text bear out what it says?

Elinor, this eldest daughter whose advice was so effectual, possessed a strength of understanding, and coolness of judgment, which qualified her, though only nineteen, to be the counsellor of her mother, and enabled her frequently to counteract, to the advantage of them all, that eagerness of mind in Mrs Dashwood which must generally have led to imprudence. She had an excellent heart; – her disposition was affectionate, and her feelings were strong; but she knew how to govern them: it was knowledge which her mother had yet to learn, and which one of her sisters had resolved never to be taught. (Chapter 1, p. 6)

The novel *appears* to confirm the firmly assertive statements offered at the beginning of the narrative. Elinor's sense, the capacity to make rational judgements based on scrupulous assessment of the evidence, seems at many points to be the dominant faculty. It is she who sees that for Marianne to accept Willoughby's gift of a horse, for instance, is not only an impropriety but an impossible expense for her mother. It is she who disapproves of the visit to Allenham. It is she who at first puts a break on their going to London during the season for financial reasons, firmly assuring Charlotte that they will not be in town. It is she who realizes that Marianne must go home after the Willoughby disaster, she who sees at the same time that to do so precipitately would be a discourtesy to Mrs Jennings. It is she who negotiates the exchange of her mother's jewellery, she who makes decisions large and small, she who effectively has most of the power in the Dashwood family of women. And she would have more were it not for her rational deference to the nominal authority of her mother as head of the family.

In tune with her aesthetic sense that beauty is utility, that a well-managed and ordered landscape betokens an ethical harmony and well-being, she conducts her practical, moral and emotional life on the same principles. Nevertheless, for all her moral scrupulousness, the world she lives in does not quite accord with these unproblematical assumptions – and it is more painful than she imagines. *Knowing* and the conduct which follows from it are not as unproblematical as she would like them to be. That sensible judgements can be made, based on a 'body of evidence' (Chapter 23, p. 117), that emotions can be made to accommodate to the reality principle, to rational evidence and to moral demands, these turn out to be presuppositions based both on ethical understanding and on the laws of probability, but not on what actually happens. The two great test cases for Elinor's rational principles are the behaviour of Willoughby and Edward, neither of which can be fully comprehended by them as sensible judgement. We have seen how Elinor insists on 'proof' and 'evidence' in both cases, and is prepared to abide by these. In different ways, this insistence leads to the 'indirection' it wishes to avoid. And indirection is symptomatic of a further skewing of knowledge. It is time to return to these two problems of passion to see how adequate are Elinor's criteria of rational sense to deal with them. Though her understanding appears to converge with that of the narrative voice, her ethics are as much an object of critique as those of other characters in the novel. They turn out to be effective when cases of practical judgement and moral conduct are concerned. They are much more limited when confronted with behaviour which falls outside the governance of pragmatism and the rules of conduct, even when these rules are interpreted with the greatest sensitivity, and even when the alertness characteristic of Elinor is exercised to its fullest extent.

In Edward's case the trajectory of guessing into which Elinor is forced is more adequate to the situation than her attempts to rationalize Willoughby. Even here she has constantly to correct herself: the hair in the ring is *not* hers; her confidence here was misplaced. Moreover, she overlooks Edward's inertia and self-pity in her conviction that it is really she who is the object of his affections. She allows his mother's unpleasant conduct to him too great a weight in excusing his own conduct to her. Her almost deterministic understanding that the 'evidence' of his engagement to Lucy at the age of nineteen constitutes a binding, virtually legal tie, prevents her from considering the duplicity of Edward's concealment of the engagement from his family. She puts excessive value on the importance of a formal tie. She is aware of 'his ill-treatment of herself' (Chapter 23, p. 117) but still does not fully consider just how equivocal it has been. His gloom over his lack of vocation, voiced in his first visit to Barton, is not fully convincing. He wants to be a clergyman, he says, but is prepared to accept his family's resistance to such a course as an alibi for not actively choosing this career. Mrs Ferrars and Fanny, with the need for vicarious experience undergone by women who are denied public power, and with the pushing, upwards mobility of the non-aristocratic wealthy classes, want him to be a great public figure, a Member of Parliament at the least. He resists this, but does nothing about pursuing his vocation. With only £2,000 he is not rich, but he has some independence.

Edward comes good in the end, forced by the crisis of the revelation of his engagement to Lucy to maintain his offer of marriage and to take active steps to become a clergyman at last. He is saved from Lucy by the luck of her preference for his brother, but not before Elinor admires the moral heroics of his stand. It conforms with her standards of moral rectitude – but for all that it is a belated stand. Throughout the narrative Edward's lack of strength and motivation forces him into a self-absorbed melancholy and Elinor into a long-term depressive condition, and no rational decision on her part to combat this ever quite succeeds. 'Her own good sense so well supported her' (p. 119), the narrative voice, ambiguously convergent with Elinor's internal debate, assures us. But events do not prove this to be so. The text constantly makes the finest discriminations to indicate the deficiences of Elinor's principles. As the depersonalizing, abstract terminology of the novel's title suggests, 'Sense' and 'Sensibility', this analysis is not conducted as a moralized account of Elinor's shortcomings: far from it; it is a painful demonstration of the rigours and constrictions, and very real damage, imposed on consciousness by a ready consent and adherence to the ideology of rational sense. When Elinor hears the news of Edward's engagement to Lucy she can scarcely stand, so overcome is she by the extraordinary news. She represses her feelings, but this lack of mercy to her emotions is not portrayed as a positive good. If Marianne is pushed towards illness, so is Elinor.

Where Willoughby is concerned Elinor is also persuaded to correct her impressions. When she overhears Willoughby using Marianne's Christian name and promising that the horse, Queen Mab, 'shall receive you', when 'you leave Barton to form your own establishment in a more lasting home', 'From that moment she doubted not of their being engaged' (Chapter 12, p. 52). But by the time Willoughby departs she has revised her assessment. True, anybody might be forgiven, including Marianne, for being deceived by these veiled euphemisms suggesting marriage, but Elinor corrects her first understanding and holds steady in her need for evidence. This turns out to be both right and limited as a policy. The romantic Mrs Dashwood upbraids her for her negativity, and though Elinor is actually right at this point, her rationality gives her a certain narrowness and pessimism when thinking of the emotions. She refuses to believe, for instance, that Colonel Brandon is a serious proposition as a replacement for Willoughby. The position of mother and daughter is reversed at the end of the novel when Mrs Dashwood argues that Marianne will recover and that she will come to see Colonel Brandon as a lover. In this case Elinor's scepticism is not justified by events.

She is overcome by Marianne's grief at Willoughby's desertion, but her inference is curiously unsupportive, based narrowly as it is on the 'evidence' of Willoughby's return of Marianne's letters in London. She comforts Marianne, protecting her from the prying eyes of Mrs Jennings and administering wine and lavender drops to her distraught sister. But when Marianne needs comfort a flinty realism refuses a recognition of her needs. 'I felt myself . . . to be as solemnly engaged to him, as if the strictest legal covenant had bound us,' Marianne laments in confusion and despair. All that Elinor can say is, 'I can believe it . . . but unfortunately he did not feel the same' (Chapter 29, p. 159). Elinor forecloses on the evidence, and confronts Marianne with an honest understanding of the truth. The truth, however, is more complex than her rather bleak, unillusioned response to experience, as we later discover from Willoughby's frantic night-time visit to the bedside of Marianne. But even if this were not so, to say 'he did not feel the same' as a form of comfort for a young woman who has just been devastated by virtual infidelity and betrayal suggests a lack of insight of a quite serious kind. Anxious and alarmed, Elinor persuades Marianne to the 'pride' (p. 160) of resistance against public shame and exhorts her to give over her wild grief 'for my mother's sake and mine' (p. 160), an ethical reminder hardly calculated to give psychological help. 'No, Marianne, in no possible way,' she replies to Marianne's appeal, 'Elinor, can he be justified?' (p. 160). Halfway between a request for confirmation of Willoughby's depravity and a request for a denial of it, she takes her sister's intense appeal at face value and offers bleak comfort. 'Exert yourself, dear Marianne,' she cries (Chapter 29, p. 156) in mingled disapproval and fear, precipitately closing down the act of mourning. Elinor's exquisite understanding of sensitive social behaviour makes her sweetly aware that she must herself drink the wine Mrs Jennings has specially opened to offer Marianne, to save giving offence when her sister cannot drink it, but Mrs Jennings is right about Marianne in a way Elinor is not – 'she had better have her cry out at once and have done with it' (p. 162). Mrs Jennings is not frightened by the demonstration of feeling.

As it is, Elinor tends to hystericize Marianne's grief. She refers to her 'nervous head-akes' to the Steeles (Chapter 32, p. 184) to prevent them invading the bedroom and to John Dashwood's comments on her sister's decline she refers to 'a nervous complaint' (Chapter 33, p. 192). These protective euphemisms of common social currency are understandable, but they do disclose not only Elinor's love but also her own inhibitions. As the intense, physical manifestations of Marianne's emotion are described, it is almost as if Elinor is herself 'nervous' about Marianne's sexuality, shocked by the body exposed in pain. Her attempts to calm Marianne's first, violent response to anguish by keeping her 'on the bed' constitute a kind of well-meaning, loving violence. It is an attempt to quell sexual pain which becomes sexual in its turn. The language of both Marianne's and Elinor's distress here is that of a spiral of arousal which ends in quiescence – the hysterical body, perhaps two hysterical bodies, as Elinor becomes caught in the same structure of emotion in response to Marianne, mimicking sexual experience. The description, 'till growing more and more hysterical', could refer to either sister.

Elinor advised her to lie down again, and for a moment she did so; but no attitude could give her ease; and in restless pain of mind and body she moved from one posture to another, till growing more and more hysterical, her sister could with difficulty keep her on the bed at all, and for some time was fearful of being constrained to call for assistance. Some lavender drops, however, which she was at length persuaded to take, were of use; and from that time till Mrs Jennings returned, she continued on the bed quiet and motionless. (Chapter 29, p. 161)

Elinor's virtually hysterical response to hysteria is significant, for her uncertain judgement here is related to the biggest mistake her rationality makes. Watching a sick patient is another form of the incessant watching which dominates this text. Elinor watches over Marianne's pain with gentle surveillance and watches over her a second time when she is ill. Guessing the body's symptoms and intuiting causes from effects is another form of deductive activity requiring scrupulous attention. The legitimate spying of the sickbed and the crucial medical judgements of the nurse are traditionally the responsibility of women: Elinor is not good at it. Almost literally fatally, she wrongly assesses the importance of Marianne's illness. Rationally in control, and believing that 'She was stronger alone' as she puts it earlier, used to power and authority and to trusting her judgement, she believes Marianne to be suffering merely from a feverish cold, and underestimates the seriousness of the illness, 'making very light of the indisposition' (Chapter 43, p. 262). Not until Marianne has a relapse and hallucinates, and well after the Palmers have left the house for fear of infection, does she send for an emergency visit from the apothecary again, and arrange for her mother to be brought from Barton. A repetition of the body movements of the earlier scene occurs. 'Marianne . . . with feverish wildness cried out:

"Is mama coming?"
"Not yet," replied the other, concealing her terror, and assisting Marianne to lie down again, "but she will be here, I hope, before it is long."' (Chapter 43, p. 263)

Elinor's over-confidence leads to another act of indirection and dishonesty, for she assures Marianne that her mother is coming before she has even sent for Mrs Dashwood. Marianne could have died without seeing her mother and without her mother having known of the seriousness of the illness until too late. The ethics of concealment and the withholding of information are brought dramatically together with acts of watching and guessing, which are the foundation of decisions to reveal or conceal information. This is a genuine test case, for it is one in which the balance of judgement is problematical. But common caution should surely have persuaded Elinor to bring her mother to Marianne. Mrs Jennings is wiser than Elinor again on this occasion. She remains behind to help with the nursing of Marianne, feeling responsible for her almost as a substitute mother, which she judges herself to be, because the two girls are under her charge. She has never been anything like so sanguine as Elinor. She 'had been inclined from the first to think Marianne's complaint more serious than Elinor' (Chapter 43, p. 260).

Mrs Jennings, however, with a kindness of heart which made Elinor really love her, declared her resolution of not stirring from Cleveland as long as Marianne remained ill, and of endeavouring, by her own attentive care, to supply to her the place of the mother she had taken her from; and Elinor found her on every occasion a most willing and active helpmate, desirous to share in all her fatigue, and often by her better experience in nursing, of material use. (Chapter 43, p. 261)

Mrs Jennings, never claiming surrogate motherhood from self-interest, is more experienced than the nineteen-year-old Elinor; over the sickbed the concerns of the novel converge; the two women work together, sharing the work of nursing and the acts of judgement it requires. And had Elinor been less certain of her independent judgement she might have acted differently. A new paradigm, however, emerges from the default of these negative circumstances. One of the solutions to the hubris of rationality in solitary judgement is the shared labour of collective watching and consultation. This emancipatory possibility emerges with the same flickering brevity with which the possibility of collective hermeneutic work on experience emerges for Marianne in the context of aesthetic judgement. The ethics of watching, guessing, knowing, judging, concealing, information-sharing and consultation are all bound up in the sickbed vigil.

It is characteristic of Jane Austen to put pressure on these moral and epistemological problems in a context where gender is important. The sickbed is women's work, and appears to confirm the gendered division of labour, limiting the emancipatory application of the text's explorations to a feminine sphere. But it is also a place where the gendered division of labour takes place on equal terms as servants and the women of the family work together. The maid takes Elinor's place when she makes arrangements to send for Mrs Dashwood. The servants tell Willoughby that Marianne is out of danger. The apothecary or doctor, Mr Harris, ostensibly the servant of the family, also meets at least as an equal at the sickbed. His presence here perhaps vindicates his profession from Anne Steele's giggling triviality when she asks to be teased about her fancy for the doctor with whom she and her sister travel to London. Men were beginning to claim authority over women at this stage in the development of the profession, particularly in midwifery and in treating 'women's' illness. The role of the doctor here, however, is neither subservient nor authoritarian. (That may be why the old-fashioned term, 'apothecary', is used.) This is not to suggest that the sickbed becomes a social idyll: but it does expose the hierarchy of the gendered division of labour by temporarily annulling it and pointing to new possibilities. The politics of the sickbed cannot be ignored.

But Elinor lacks something. Her rationality is shown to be deficient. Sensitive and conscientious though she is, her judgements are almost disastrous at a point where good judgement is literally a matter of life and death. To see what this lack is we have to go back to Johnson's definition of sense. Elinor certainly possesses 'strength of natural reason' and 'moral perception'. She is quick and alert, but she lacks *sense*, or rather, cannot trust sense, in the fundamental physiological form defined in two ways by Johnson; 'Faculty or power by which external objects are perceived; the sight; touch; hearing; smell'. 'Perception by the senses; sensation.' Everyone, of course, experiences sense data and possesses faculties for perceiving sense data. Without this one would experience nothing at all. But Elinor's faculties of 'sense' in this understanding of the term seem underdeveloped or limited. She ignores, or is sceptical of, sensory experience. Suspicious of Marianne's sensuous response to landscape, sceptically demanding 'evidence' as empirical guarantor of judgement, her response to the body in sexual anguish or in illness is symptomatic of her distrust of the sensory in her own and other people's lives. Elinor's rational and social project, a necessary project indeed, is the constant watching and assessment of the unknown other. But Johnson reminds us that sense has its roots in sensation, in seeing, touching, hearing, smelling. It is through the sensory that responsiveness to the objects of the external world and a full awareness of them can be developed. The sickbed is, again, a test case, for it requires an alertness of the senses to physical signs, a sensory response to the sensory experience of others and a highly developed capacity for seeing, hearing, touching.

Her failure to respond to the evidence of other people's bodies means that Elinor misreads Marianne's needs at a profounder level. She tries to be a mother to Marianne in her sickness when Marianne is actually longing for her real mother. It is characteristic of Jane Austen's writing that this insight does not stop at a moral and psychological understanding of Elinor's relationship with Marianne. The judgement and 'sense' of her text is searchingly, scrupulously, open. Through this relationship she asks a question fundamental to 'sentimental' readings of the self and engages in a philosophical problem which is at the heart of the culture of sentiment and sensibility. Is it possible to get inside other people's bodies – and minds – at all? Through Marianne's illness she evokes an eighteenth-century debate which has been incipient in her text throughout, and in doing so complicates further the relation between sense and sensibility, breaking down the antithesis between them. Correspondingly, the relation between the two girls is also complicated further.

The axiom of sentimental experience is that it is capable not simply of intense feeling but of sympathy. That is, consciousness has the capacity to respond to the situation of the subjectivity outside itself through projecting itself into the experience of that external subjectivity. This movement out of the self constitutes the bonds of social feeling because it presupposes and strengthens an affinity between human experiences which enables empathy to occur. From Shaftesbury onwards, the morality of the sentimental experience is predicated on this act of changing places with another and the assumption of the essential *sameness* of people, despite the differences of gender and social class. The ethical depends on psychological understanding. From this benevolence, compassion, and the social virtues flow. In *Characteristics* (1711), Shaftesbury wrote of the 'Pleasures of *Sympathy* or *Participation with others'.*[5] By the time Adam Smith wrote his *The Theory of Moral Sentiments* (1759), this interpretation of sympathy had strengthened to the capacity to intuit physical experience and to get inside someone else's body. Moral understanding depends on the imagination and on 'changing places in fancy' with another person: 'we enter as it were into his body, and become in some measure the same person with him, and thence form some idea of his sensations, and even feel something which, though weaker in degree, is not altogether unlike them'.[6] For Shaftesbury, sympathy was virtually a sixth 'moral sense', but this moral sense had to be founded on the essential knowableness of others and of the world. With the idea of sympathy we are back with the problem of *knowing* with which this chapter began.

For the idea of sympathy to work we have to assume, as a later philosopher, Thomas Reid, was to put it, 'an invincible belief in the existence of external objects'.[7] In order to assume the affinities and common experiences upon which sympathy is founded, a prior assent to the stable, empirical existence of external bodies must be given, or at least to the stability of sense data. It is on this point that a fissure in British empiral philosophy occurs. Jane Austen's novel, one might say, is written across the gap created by an intellectual split. To see how this is the case some details of this split are required. The essentials of the argument between Thomas Reid, who has just been mentioned, and David Hume, need to be discussed.

To begin with Reid: he responded with emphatic denial to Hume's sceptical proposition that, because external objects are necessarily represented in our minds by ideas, we cannot guarantee the existence of those objects. Reid constantly made appeals to 'the universal sense of man', the 'plain man' and to 'what every man of common sense knows', in order to argue (sometimes with considerable power) for a philosophical justification of self-evident premises rather than for the scepticism to be found in Hume:

If a plain man, uninstructed in philosophy, has faith to receive these mysteries, how great must be his astonishment! He is brought into a new world, where everything he sees, tastes, or touches, is an idea – a fleeting kind of being which he can conjure into existence, or can annihilate in the twinkling of an eye.

After his mind is somewhat composed, it will be natural for him to ask his philosophical instructor, Pray, sir, are there then no substantial and permanent beings called the sun and moon, which continue to exist whether we think of them or not? . . .

[Hume] would assure the querist that it is a vulgar error, a mere prejudice of the ignorant and unlearned, to think that there are any permanent and substantial beings called the sun and the moon; that the heavenly bodies, our own bodies, and all bodies whatsoever, are nothing but ideas in our minds . . . nay, says Mr Hume, there is nothing in nature but ideas only; for what we call a mind is nothing but a train of ideas connected by certain relations between themselves. (*On the Intellectual Powers of Man,* 1785)[8]

The methods by which Reid attempts to refute Hume, and to restore that matching correlation between perception and objects with a separate existence, are less important here than his resistance to Hume. It was vital to him to argue for a stable universe in which ideas in the mind betokened pre-existing objects. For Hume, on the other hand, to assert that nothing but images are present in the mind is to obey 'the obvious dictates of reason':

and no man who reflects ever doubted that the existences which we consider, when we say *this house* and *that tree*, are nothing but perceptions in the mind, and fleeting copies and representations of other existences, which remain uniform and independent. So far, then, we are necessitated, by reasoning, to depart from the primary instincts of nature, and to embrace a new system with regard to the evidence of our senses.[9]

It is significant that, though Hume invokes the concept of sympathy in considering ethical relations, it is precisely the weakness and limits of sympathy to which he draws attention. The scepticism about what Reid calls 'all bodies whatsoever', issues in a solipsistic account of sympathy. For if other existences are fleeting copies known by the mind, the feelings discovered in the act of projection are likely to turn out to be aspects of our own narcissism, an inverse form of sympathy, rather than the act of changing places with another which is the foundation of sentimental ethics. For Hume sympathy arises only from the 'immediate connexion' of a person with its object:

And tho' this advantage or harm be often very remote from ourselves, yet sometimes 'tis very near us, and interests us strongly by sympathy. This concern we readily extend to other cases, that are resembling; and when these are very remote, our sympathy is proportionably weaker, and our praise or blame fainter and more doubtful. The case is here the same as in our judgments concerning external bodies. All objects seem to diminish by their distance.[10]

A 'sympathy with persons remote from us' is 'much fainter than with persons near and contiguous', Hume added.

His understanding of the weakness of sympathy, then, rests on an epistemological position profoundly different from the common-sense philosophy which later challenged his thought. All Hume would allow as the basis of knowledge was the capacity of consciousness to make connections between different moments of experience in time, but not that it made inferences from externally existing phenomena. You can only know what is in your mind, not that anything may exist outside it. And, in a section of *A Treatise of Human Nature* (1739) entitled 'Of scepticism with regard to the senses', he reiterated the thesis developed throughout the *Treatise*, that the coherence and constancy of external bodies, and the inferences we make from cause and effect, are built up by the 'connexions', a word he uses constantly, established in our minds by the association of ideas based on recurrent experience. It is the mind which constructs relations by extrapolating contiguity and continuity from past experience: it is able to 'connect' past and present occurrences because it relies on 'the regular succession of these perceptions'. But these inferences are not guaranteed by a pre-existing world.

To return to *Sense and Sensibility* and to Elinor's dilemmas in the sickroom, how does this detour into Reid and Hume help to situate the novel's concerns? One might expect Elinor's powerful rationality to align her with the conservative, stabilizing, common-sense views of Reid. The certainty of the permanent existence of external objects, the capacity of the mind to comprehend them and correlate perception and objects would accord with her sense of order and the need to make rational meaning out of experience, one would think. However, the common-sense permanence and knowableness of objects guarantees that very morality of excessive affect which Elinor distrusts: it enables that projection into the very body of the other through empathy, or 'sympathy', which is the basis of sentimental morality. In the crisis of the sickroom a capacity for 'changing places in fancy' might have helped her, but she draws back from this ultimate move out of the self. Her scrupulous behavioural skills, always aware of the need to prevent the giving of offence or of hurting feelings – we remember her smiling offer to drink Mrs Jennings' specially opened wine – tend in the direction of Reid rather than the self-interested narcissism of Hume, but they are less projections of feeling than minutely observant acts of judgement. Reid is refused because empathy and sympathy are not regarded as the basis of moral experience. Elinor resists the morality of empathy and so does the text.

It seems at times that both Elinor, and the text, *want* the reassuring stability of the Reidian paradigm, yet Elinor's very need for 'evidence' turns her into a sceptical Humean. For the common-sense school makes self-evident all that her scrupulousness calls into question. It is because she cannot enter into the minds and bodies of those who confound and puzzle her – Marianne, Willoughby and Edward – that she dwells so sceptically on the meaning of their actions. For the sentimental Mrs Dashwood, who declares her love for both Willoughby and Edward so precipitately, Marianne's actions are self-evident, but she is wrong about this self-evidence. For Elinor, such immediate projection of feeling is inappropriate. It forecloses and replaces judgement, scrutiny, and reflection. The two models of experience are mutually exclusive, but, more importantly, empathy doesn't work. If we are ever in doubt that this is a Humean novel, it is only necessary to remember Fanny and John Dashwood's coldness and failure of empathy at the beginning of the novel to see this. Utter self-interest and failure of empathy is the other side of sentimental sympathy. The John Dashwoods rationalize their 'remote' connection, as Hume terms it, with their family, even though they live in the same house, in order not to feel sympathy. True, the text has longings for common sense reassurance, but the Humean model constantly refuses these needs.

Rather than forming two sides of a neat epistemological opposition, between common sense (Reid and Elinor) and narcissistic sensibility (Hume and Marianne) the two girls seem more like two forms of a split, Humean subjectivity searching for meaning in a world where the contradictions of psychologizing bourgeois sentimentality, its specious warmth, and its terrible coldness, are everywhere apparent. For Hume's scepticism requires sensibility as well as sense. In order for his model of mind to work Hume has to suppose a double experience, one experience resembling or repeating the other in our understanding. Impressions, the first awareness of experience in our minds, and consonant with feeling, are mediated by ideas, consonant with thought. Memory keeps impressions alive, with a 'vivacity' which sustains their immediacy. Imagination doubles memory but reproduces experience in thought in a weakened and more abstract form (Book I, Part I, Section I). The hierarchical imagination has to double the wayward impression because this is the only way of sustaining the 'connexion' or association of ideas (Book I, Part I, Section IV). The relations between impressions are kept in place by the imagination which perceives and sustains resemblances through contiguity in time and space and through relations of recurrence, which suggest cause and effect. The imagination does not *always* or invariably repeat the same connections, for that would mean a life of constant repetition. There would be no change, no probabilities or possibilities, which are the essence of change and of choice. Nor do connections necessarily *always* occur under imagination's rule, for that would remove the spontaneity and vivacity of the experience of the association of ideas. This is a risky epistemology.

Elinor and Marianne, one dominated by thought, the other by feeling, seem to represent the severed halves of impression and idea, memory and imagination. The Humean universe depends upon a situation which is always in danger of falling apart, the doubling of expression and idea, thought and feeling. And to the extent that experience is always veering between this perpetual repetition and perpetual arbitrariness, it is an incoherent universe. How is experience kept together? By chance, it seems, rather than choice. The only guarantee of its coherence depends upon making the right connections. Interestingly, Hume cites the 'connexions' of the extended family to illustrate what he means by the 'relations', which sustain and order experience in his section on 'Of the Connexion or Association of Ideas'.

That we may understand the full extent of these relations, we must consider, that two objects are connected together in the imagination, not only when the one is immediately resembling, contiguous to, or the cause of the other, but also when there is interposed betwixt them a third object, which bears to both of them any of these relations [i.e. resembles them]. This may be carried on to a great length; tho' at the same time we may observe, that each remove considerably weakens the relation. Cousins in the fourth degree are connected by *causation*, if I may be allowed to use that term; but not so closely as brothers, much less child and parent. In general we may observe, that all the relations of blood depend upon cause and effect, and are esteemed near or remote, according to the number of connecting causes interpos'd betwixt the persons. (Book I, Part I, Section IV)[11]

Fascinatingly, the persistent language of cousins and brothers, of near and remote relations, which is so marked in *Sense and Sensibility*, appears at a crucial point in Hume's *Treatise*. 'Chance alone wou'd join them', he writes of the hypothesis that ideas might be 'entirely loose and unconnected' (Book I, Part I, Section IV). The metaphor of the family enables him to suggest that there *are* relations of resemblance, contiguity and cause and effect in our experience. But this assertion of relationship relies on a sleight of hand, or, rather, a pun or euphemism. Family relations are connected by 'causation', that is, by the sexual act which creates biological blood relations in the extended family tree, 'if I may be allowed to use that term'. Hume is assuming that perception works in the same way, classifying experiences into connected groups, with ever more tenuous category affinities the more remote relations are. But this is to make connections far more certain than they are: sexual affiliations and category affinities do not really work in the same way unless we take the metaphor of the family literally. And Hume is guilty of this here. Later he is to say that causation is a matter of recurrence and *probable* recurrence, rather than the product of intrinsic, rule-bound situations, where relationship of cause and effect is always inevitable, never arbitrary and always lucid (Book I, Part II, Section IV). This description twists back upon the metaphor of the family and makes it insecure in its turn. It suggests first, that the same conditions of probability and recurrence govern family relations: second, that these relations are constructed rather than intrinsic. That is, both in family relations and perception there is an element of *chance*. As if aware of the mystification and tenuousness of his metaphor he writes later that marriage ensures the passing on of property because it limits women's sexuality, preventing the child of an unknown father from inheriting property illegitimately (Book III, Part II, Section XII). Hume is caught up in the same problems as Jane Austen's text.

It is interesting that 'connections' in the association of ideas and 'connections' in terms of family relationships converge in Hume's text and Jane Austen's. Nothing appears to guarantee 'connection', in the mind, or in social arrangements. Elinor and Marianne are at the mercy of other people's accounts of the family 'connection', as we have seen. To take life into their own hands they have to attempt to make this dissolving world coherent by making the right mental, perceptual connections at least. Arguably, Hume's ungrounded, doubled world prepares the way for the new free trading mercantilism of the late-eighteenth century. We have already seen how one model of the family presages this openness by asserting an almost infinite set of interdependencies and connections. The free and open structures of connection and devolved connection upon which free trade depends open up in his work. The release of exchange value from intrinsically fixed relations, another requirement of capital, opens up in his sceptical refusal to correlate internal and internal. The creation of a system which can abstract the particular to facilitate exchange, and yet retain the immediacy of sensory awareness to facilitate consumption, is another aspect of the Hume universe.[12] As women, seemingly excluded from these new relations, yet organized by them, Elinor and Marianne are symptomatic of the divided Hume consciousness. Living respectively through idea and impression, abstraction and intensity, imagination and memory, they each discover the limits of their experience. And perhaps another piece of *Hamlet* falls into place in the text, as each lives, like Ophelia, a 'divided' self, as Claudius has it (IV v 82). They live at a point when the hierarchies of aristocratic connection are giving way to the possessive individualism which facilitates entrepreneurial 'connexion', but they are at home in neither.

Elinor's hopes of a world of rational recurrence and inference are rarely confirmed, and, as we have seen, her scepticism drives her to revise and re-order experience, to a perpetual attempt to correlate actions and words, and to trust very little without 'evidence'. Perhaps the peak of Humean experience for her is the moment when Lucy reveals her engagement to Edward. 'We cannot mean the same Mr Ferrars,' she says, certain that there has been a mistake. Lucy's 'We can mean no other', refuses that certainty (Chapter 22, p. 111). Yet for Elinor, Edward's conduct has been so uncharacteristic that it cannot come under the rubric of recurrence and continuity in time or even in place – unknown to her he has had connections in Plymouth all along. That is why the moment is so shocking. Elinor imagines that there must be *two* Edwards for a moment, as the only way of explaining the breach of probability. In a sense she is right. There *are* two Edwards, 'entirely loose and unconnected', because he is leading a double life, and has been doing so for a number of years. One of the problems of Hume's epistemology is the continuity of identity, for if experience is made up of discontinuous, fleeting moments, continuity is hard to assert. This is a poignant moment for Elinor, when she has to give up Edward's consistency with his love. The two, indeed, are bound up with one another. In a quieter way the moment is as intense as Marianne's loss.

For both Elinor and Marianne the inconsistency of the men they love makes them feel that they must have been acting a part and simulating affection. Elinor's task has to be the exact opposite of Marianne's, to preserve the vitality of impulse, while Marianne struggles towards control. We have already seen how the life of impulse is so harshly checked for Marianne. Before moving on to the last aspect of the breakdown of connections between words and actions it is as well to remember the strengths of Marianne's intensity and consent to the life of impressions. For commentators tend to be harsh on her 'revolutionary' temperament, on her histrionics, and on the solipsism which makes her brood at the piano, oblivious of the social world. There is a moment when her warmth and vivacity is genuinely energizing, when it kindles moral feeling as well as moral duty. It is the supremely embarrassing moment when Elinor and Lucy are together in London and are unexpectedly visited by Edward. Marianne, quite unaware that Lucy is secretly engaged to Edward or that Elinor knows this, bursts out in praise of Edward's rectitude. Not noticing, either, that Lucy has sneered at her when commenting on her seeming lack of faith in young men's capacity to keep engagements, she springs not to her own defence but to Edward's with a mixture of high generosity and obtuseness:

'Not so, indeed; for, seriously speaking, I am very sure that conscience only kept Edward from Harley Street. And I really believe he *has* the most delicate conscience in the world; the most scrupulous in performing every engagement however minute, and however it may make against his interest or pleasure. He is the most fearful of giving pain, of wounding expectation, and the most incapable of being selfish of any body I ever saw. Edward, it is so and I will say it.' (Chapter 35, p. 205)

There are multiple ironies here, many more than Marianne's unconscious pun on engagement, which I shall consider again, but for the moment it is important to remember that the intensity of her commendation has predictive force. The vivacity of her argument, which Hume valued because we must feel to think, clearly shames Edward at that moment but might well have ensured that in the crisis of the revelation of his secret, he *did* sustain his engagement, connecting his past with his present, and bringing about that consistency and recurrence which sustains the chancy Hume universe. Conscience, of course, *did* keep Edward from Harley Street, but not for the reasons Marianne is thinking of – he was too compromised to meet Elinor. Humean misprision is the stuff of comedy. Energy and warmth drive moral feeling here, by making it vivid, rather than the other way round. The meaning of scrupulousness comes alive for Marianne, and perhaps for Edward too. Earlier Edward has said of Marianne that, 'I have always set her down as a lively girl' (Chapter 17, p. 82), and Elinor corrects him by distinguishing between the difference between a 'merry' temperament and the 'animation' possessed by Marianne. Here animation pays off.

So far, then, I have considered the necessities of watching, the problems of knowing and the inferential activity, with its accompanying indirection and deviousness, which follows from Jane Austen's social world. Spying, nursing, aesthetic spectatorship, all become analogues for those forms of social watching which are a necessity given the conditions of this world. That she moves towards the sceptical, chancy, insecure model of knowledge provided by Hume, with its constant perceptual risks, is partly explained by the way that other, common-sense models of knowledge and feeling invoke sentimental empathy as the basis of understanding, something ultimately rejected in her texts. Willoughby, who appears to identify so deeply with Marianne and Mrs Dashwood, is a demonstration of the fallacy, the essential callousness, of feeling, as the basis of action. He belongs to the suspect psychology of 'attachment' rather than to the epistemology of 'connection'. The advantage of a sceptical understanding of experience is that it accepts a more mobile world, however insecure that world is. But it becomes crucial to make the right connections in a world where the arbitrariness and mobility of social structures and perceptual experience seem to mimic each other, where social organization and the association of ideas, epistemology and society, can both be described in terms of family relationship which turn out to be insecure terms. To get your inferences right, or to adapt them resourcefully, is a mode of survival. To 'match' words and actions correctly is crucial. Whether consciously or not, Jane Austen's text draws together the vocabulary of filiation in both *Hamlet* and Hume – cousin, brother – to explore this structure of uncertain connection. The brilliance of making *Hamlet* an undertext is that its dark, brooding complexities can be invoked and yet kept at bay by comedy: the tragic structures are transposed and re-inflected in the lucid sharpness of satire, irony and pun.

The incipient insecurity of the world of sceptical experience is built into the text not only at the psychological level but also structurally as an aspect of narrative experience. People are mysterious to one another, we have seen, even to themselves. Fanny Dashwood veers into ambiguity when she speaks of the minimal obligations she and her husband have to the Dashwood women as a matter of 'sending them presents of fish and game, and so forth, whenever they are in season' (Chapter 2, p. 10). The ambiguity discloses even more than the conflation between the Dashwood women and game, already discussed, which puts them on the same level as creatures who can be eliminated: the phrase, 'when they are in season' applies as much to animals as to the female Dashwoods, and for a moment opens up an importunate, animal sexuality in the Dashwood women, betraying Fanny's sense that their sexuality and their ability to reproduce are a threat to her. It is not surprising that the slang word, 'monstrous', should be significant in the text, subliminally suggesting something unnatural as well as the intended adverbial meaning, hugely. The chancy nature of language, where inadvertent ambiguity resists control, is as much a feature of a Humean comedy as misprision. A 'monstrous' language, where categories are illegitimately connected is always a linguistic possibility in a world of chance relations.

Because scepticism questions the natural, what is unnatural becomes a problem. We have seen the hovering allusions to incest, that 'monstrous' or unnatural relationship, in *Sense and Sensibility*. In a sceptical reading of experience, what is a 'correct' or legitimate connection is not self-evident, because it is likely that this will be constructed by custom and thus will be contingent rather than necessary. Sir John Middleton and Mrs Jennings, Mrs Dashwood and Willoughby and Edward, about both of whom she uses the word 'love', are the 'obvious' incestuous relations along with those of Robert Ferrars and Colonel Brandon's brother. But the text is oddly indeterminate about the nature of people's relations to one another in many ways. We do not really know, for instance, what form of cousinship Sir John bears to Mrs Dashwood. Usually so scrupulous in documenting connections, the text is silent here, as if mooting another problematic situation of contiguity or distance. They are about the same age, and supposedly the children of brothers or sisters: but was Mrs Dashwood a Middleton before marriage? Is she a first or second cousin? The loose identification of cousin here (which Hume takes to the fourth remove) is one of those small, unsettling irritants to the stability of things of which the text is so full.

Similarly, almost until the last, a union of Colonel Brandon with Mrs Dashwood or with Elinor is not ruled out. Mrs Jennings, indeed, suspects the latter. Both Brandon and Willoughby are at a 'remove', as the language of family relationship and of Hume has it, from Marianne, and use Elinor as an intermediary in their communications. There is an ambiguous sexual charge in both relations. Willoughby's designation of Elinor as 'saucy' when she argues with him about Brandon's character (Chapter 10, p. 45) suggests the antagonism of sexual attraction, and the intensity of his confessional passion and his desire to be thought well of, at Cleveland, includes Elinor. In the same way, Colonel Brandon's confessional intensity during the story of his ward's tragedy is curiously lover-like. Elinor has the dreamwork satisfaction of being the object of her sister's lovers' attention. She wants Edward in the world of the reality principle, but she is given power over the other men too at a deeper level and in a necessarily unresolved way.

The strangely scandalous possibilities lurking in the text create the narrative intensity which comes of such openness and such unresolved denial of closure. It is a way of persuading the reader to undergo the experience of living out the possibility, in the act of reading itself, that 'chance alone wou'd join' (Hume) people to one another. This narrative rhythm moves us from psychology to the structure of the novel, and to my last point about its organization.

Because the text is so rigorously concerned with the unknowableness of other people and the unpredictability of events, refusing the fantasy of identification and certainty, the novel is organized round the epistemology of scepticism through its narrative structure. Repeatedly, encounters occur where misprision and incomplete knowledge, often on the part of several people, dictate behaviour. Sometimes the reader knows this only after the episode is well over; sometimes the comedy enables only the reader to know what is really the case. This playing with perception and at revealing and concealing knowledge makes the reader's position as judge, spy and aesthetic spectator as problematic as those of the characters in the novel. It is a comic ploy of great subtlety, but it is also a way of ensuring that the certainty of knowledge is never seen as straightforward. The indirection of knowing goes deep, arising both from the necessity 'of telling lies when politeness required it', as Elinor is forced to do (Chapter 21, p. 104), and from the subtlest contradictions of experience. Not until Henry James's work carried the multiple disjunctions in knowing to a new order of epistemological complexity does the novel reach this kind of perceptual sublety again.

We have seen how people speculate about one another directly, Marianne wondering at the coldness of the last adieus of Edward and Elinor, Elinor reciprocally wondering about her sister's engagement. There are clear examples of the duping of the self by desire or by deception. The hair in Edward's ring, which Elinor is certain is her own, is a case in point. One of the climaxes of the novel manifests itself as a shocking break in coherent connections, as expectations break down. Elinor's relief that her mother's carriage may be arriving at Cleveland to support the sick Marianne at last is shockingly contradicted by the unexpected arrival of Willoughby. And, of course, Fanny and John Dashwood, the latter a male gossip, are brazenly, wonderfully duped by Lucy. But the structural misprision I have in mind is rather different. It happens when two or more absolutely different kinds of coherence are being made simultaneously by two or more people. For the point being made is not the nihilistic one that we don't, or can't, know about the world: it is more that different people make different coherences according to their position in relation to one another. The Humean desire (and it *is* a desire however sceptically conceived) for consistency, coherence and recurrence, rather like Freud's account of the needs of the death wish for repetition, is what drives people to the will to order. And the will to order is what drives people to misprision. Misprision is an inverted form of deception, so to speak. An example of this is Edward's exclamation when Mrs Dashwood tells him that they are moving to Devonshire:

Edward turned hastily towards her, on hearing this, and, in a voice of surprise and concern, which required no explanation to her, repeated, 'Devonshire! Are you, indeed, going there? So far from hence! And to what part of it?' (Chapter 5, p. 21)

Mrs Dashwood, and presumably the listening Elinor, believe that he is distressed because Elinor is going far away: in reality he is disturbed because they are getting so *near* to his secret. His enquiry about the part of Devonshire where they intend to settle is not motivated by the sense of loss or even by politeness: they might after all be going to the very place in which the Steeles live, Plymouth. The reader is not in a position to know the facts either. Lucy's disclosure is made so much later that the reader is likely to have forgotten the incident by then. But in what sense could Edward be said to be 'feigning' here, an act from which Elinor later exonerates him?

Similar to this is Mrs Jennings's brilliant intuitive guess about Elinor's Norland lover. 'He is the curate of the parish I dare say' (Chapter 12, p. 54). She is not right, and in guessing she is making inferences from Elinor's temperament and from her cottage-dwelling position low in the scale of social class (as curates were also), thus offering an implied insult to the girl. The listening Elinor does not yet know of Edward's aspirations to become a clergyman. At this point in the novel she would remember his high class position and gentlemanly status in the rich, upwardly mobile Ferrars family. Another such instance of double understanding occurs when Willoughby says his farewells at the cottage. 'I will not torment myself any longer by remaining among friends whose society it is impossible for me now to enjoy' (Chapter 15, p. 67). 'Impossible' has a greater weight for him than for the Dashwoods. He means that he can never see them again – because his hopes of the Smith inheritance have been dashed, because he must find a rich woman to marry, and also because he is vulnerable to the more public discovery of his seduction of Eliza Williams, and thus to the moral censure which would ensue, making him socially unacceptable, particularly to friends of Colonel Brandon. All these conditions dictate his 'impossible'. But to the unsuspecting Dashwoods he has been compelled to go by some irrational authoritarian edict to which Mrs Dashwood attempts to give coherence, by romantically positing a forbidden romance, and getting it wrong. He is saying goodbye for ever but they do not suspect that he is. Neither the reader nor the Dashwoods can know that this is the case until much later.

This, Willoughby's ambiguous account of his reasons for going and his vagueness about returning, is why another subtle misprision occurs, perhaps one of the most poignantly comic in the novel. Out walking, the girls see 'a man on horseback riding towards them' and 'distinguish him to be a gentleman' (because of the servant accompanying him, not mentioned until later?) (Chapter 16, p. 75). Marianne rushes towards him, certain that it is Willoughby: 'His air, his coat, his horse', a surprising statement, given her great reservations about the man it really is, Edward. 'I knew how soon he would come,' she says, her sight obeying her desire (p. 75). Elinor checks her: 'It is not Willoughby', but she insists that it is (p. 75). There is a slight time-lag before we are told that the man is Edward, and we realize that Elinor has recognized Edward well before Marianne has mistaken him for Willoughby. Marianne does not realize this because Elinor not only protects her from the embarrassment of showing publicly that this is not the man she wants, but is also concealing the same emotions that Marianne is openly expressing, almost as if stealing her sister's emotion. The quickened perceptions of love are operating in both cases, recognizing a familiar figure and rapidly constructing a coherent narrative from this, but one girl is right and the other wrong, and the girl who is right is embarrassed by being so as much as Marianne is embarassed by being wrong. The fullness of this delicate negotiation with misprision is known only to the reader. It is partly a lesson in the wilful reading of the semiotic marks of class and gender – 'distinguish him to be a gentleman' – but the subtlety goes further. What it does is to emphasize the element of fictional coherence in experience by confronting the reader of fiction with a demonstration of the desire for coherence, a desire fiction invites. The will to order is an aspect of writing and reading as well as the need of the characters in the text.

The two grand instances of multiple misprision in the text are the meeting between Elinor, Lucy, Edward and Marianne, and Mrs Jennings's mistake about Elinor's marriage. In one case the reader knows the complexities of the situation, in the second she or he does not. In one case the reader is in some kind of hermeneutic control, in the second case hermeneutic mastery is deliberately withheld, and the reader is disempowered, coming to knowledge circuitously. Sometimes the reader is put, as it were, behind the arras, sometimes she or he is positioned almost as one of the social group who make up Jane Austen's small interpretative communities. For what you can make of your world is partly a matter of desire, a form of hermeneutic erotics, partly the result of *agreement* on meaning, and partly a matter of power. Where you are positioned at any point can privilege your insight and empower understanding – or take it away.

When Edward enters the room where Elinor and Lucy are sitting, all look foolish. But Edward does not know that Elinor knows of his engagement to Lucy, or that Lucy knows Elinor knows. Elinor and Lucy know that he does not know. They become 'witnesses' to his discomfort – the term almost has legal force. Marianne appears, fetched by Elinor after an interval when Edward and Lucy are left alone, about which the text is completely silent (what, after all, Hume asked, if anything, goes on in the world when one is not there?). Marianne behaves like 'a sister', clearly anticipating Edward's marriage to Elinor (Chapter 35, p. 204). She is warmly proprietory, gazing in delight at Elinor and Edward, only regretting that 'their delight in each other should be checked by Lucy's unwelcome presence', and making it clear that she feels this. She even whispers to Edward that Lucy cannot stay long when he is about to go, not realizing that he is longing to get away. Not knowing anything of the secret engagement or of Elinor's knowledge of it, she simply fails to read the signs with a grand obliviousness. Everything she says must almost inevitably be grossly tactless to almost everybody and *must* have the force of innuendo, but innuendo with a different meaning for everyone, without her knowing it. 'You are what you always were!' (p. 205) she says to Edward, with lavish warmth: always the honourable man she thinks him, always, to the wincing Edward, the man engaged to Lucy, a secret he has always wanted to conceal; but to Elinor, always the unfaithful, inconsistent man, and to Lucy always the unwilling fiancé whose relation to her she is longing to reveal. For a moment there are as many Edwards as there are people in the room. Marianne's warmth carries her further into trouble, assuming that Edward will accompany them home to Barton, and interpreting his confusion as a sign of his love for Elinor, tactlessly complaining of the terrible Dashwood dinner party (given by his own sister), and forcing an explanation for his absence which leads to Lucy's cruel pun on 'engagements' – for after all, this is the word that is on her mind in a different sense. Oddly, the intense complexities of the situation make Marianne seem slightly crazed, whereas her behaviour could not be more appropriate to a warm social occasion. It is the knowledge and complicity of *other people* who force this upon her by making her an outsider to their secrets. Deprived of norms without knowing it, assuming relationships that do not exist, and taking for granted the natural superiority of the Dashwood family, her class prejudice against Lucy is all the more tellingly exposed. It is a wonderful way of indicating the existence of power structures which are not upheld by the circumstances in which they exist. Marianne's coherences are wide of the mark.

The grand finale of misprision occurs when Mrs Jennings, Polonius behind the arras, hears Colonel Brandon offering Edward the Delaford living via Elinor and thinks that he is proposing marriage. The desire for the match is co-extensive with that hermeneutic 'matching' of words and actions which forces Mrs Jennings to 'consistent' conclusions ever more inconsistent with the facts. This time the reader is not, as it were, in the drawing room but positioned behind the arras with the listener who gains power over the couple by hearing them without their knowledge. Cheerful, generous, superficial and prolix, Mrs Jennings is the first detective in British fiction because she enjoys the powers of hidden surveillance and the master–slave relation this brings with it. The reader, not given the facts until after the reported misprision, is in puzzled collusion with her. The words of the couple by the window, 'I am afraid it cannot take place very soon' (Colonel Brandon), elicit from Mrs Jennings the puzzled aside, 'sure he need not wait to be older': 'I shall always think myself very much obliged to you' (Elinor) elicits the delight of confirmation (Chapter 39, p. 238). The Colonel is speaking of Edward's postponed marriage to Lucy, not of his own, and Mrs Jennings fits Edward into the picture by assuming that he is to officiate at the marriage and that the long wait is caused by the need for his ordination. The elaborate, circuitous and inherently unlikely forms of explanation required to make the facts fit the interpretation suggest brilliantly the indirection not only of spying itself, but of the wild surmise it resorts to for 'coherence'.

In this case the interpretation is changed to fit the facts. In Marianne's case the facts are altered to fit the interpretation. But both suggest, through the social politics of everyday life, how knowledge is a *social* matter, depending on agreement and openness. Elinor admits to Edward that she is constantly revising her judgements, deliberating what people say about themselves and 'what other people say of them' (Chapter 17, p. 82). Reading of this kind sustains the social world, and the novel's reader is trained in this difficult and tricky process throughout. Jane Austen's novels do not remain enthralled with indirection and the hermeneutic impossibilities which were later to be exploited in the epistemological complexities of the novels of Henry James. Neither is she deceived into believing that wholly undistorted communication is possible in the stratified society of the late-eighteenth and early-nineteenth centuries. But the drive to make *sense* in Johnson's sixth and tenth meanings of the word, 'Reason; reasonable meaning' (coherence), 'Meaning, import' (signification), is a social drive for agreement. Coherence and signification are often at variance, that is what creates the comedy of Marianne's sublime misprision and Mrs Jennings's grotesque misinterpretation. Perhaps they always will be. Nevertheless, the work required to bring coherence and signification together is social work, as in the cottage community of women, or in the conversations on the aesthetic which occur in that environment.

Despite its narrow stairs this is an idealized community and thus an unlikely model. It is the only one, for instance, in which we see humane communication with servants, who, we remember, express joy at the arrival of the women. By its nature, because it can't reproduce itself without men, it is impossible to sustain. And even here linguistic confusion occurs. Significantly, the manservant who says, 'I suppose you know, ma'am, that Mr Ferrars is married', inducing the pallor of Elinor and the hysterics of Marianne, creates confusion by using the strict upper-class form of words for the eldest son, which Robert Ferrars now technically is (Chapter 47, p. 299). And even in this comparative idyll of communication, Marianne feels a lack: 'sometimes I have kept my feelings to myself, because I could find no language to describe them in but what was worn and hackneyed out of all sense and meaning' (Chapter 18, p. 85). The need for the renewal of language, for new 'sense and meaning', is hinted here. But Marianne's feeling of linguistic solipsism remains unanswered in the novel.

Since the community of *Sense and Sensibility* is not adept at language making, as the 'monstrous' slang of the Steeles, Charlotte and Sir John Middleton suggests, the text itself prefers to work with tonic lucidity, leaving much unsaid. Reversing the habits of *Hamlet*, where there is more art than matter (II ii 96), it prefers to work with spare economy of language. The only person who does not use such economy is the garrulous Jennings–Polonius, who floods the text with words and linguistic vitality. It is from her that one discovers the magnificence of Delaford, with its stewponds, the mulberry trees where 'Charlotte and I did stuff' (Chapter 30, p. 166), and the carriages to be seen passing on the public road (another reference to *Columella*). But it is also through her ever-created flow of language that the blanks in the text are most conspicious. In the episodes of misprision I have been looking at, the presumption is that through the exercise of judgement a shared if provisional coherence might ultimately be arrived at as consensual social negotiations continue; the interpretative process is possible. The blanks exposed by Mrs Jennings's talk, however, are not those to which the civil process of revisionary judgement, of matching words to actions, is relevant. The gaps in the text are much more like those picturesque gaps which challenge by almost defying understanding.

It is Mrs Jennings who takes the main part in goading Margaret into revealing the 'secret' of Elinor's 'Curate'. It is also she who reminds us of Marianne's future responsibilities: 'Two thousand a-year without debt or drawback – except the little love-child, indeed; aye, I had forgot her; but she may be 'prenticed out at small cost, then what does it signify?' (Chapter 30, p. 166). Margaret, the third sister about whom almost nothing is known, and the 'love-child', or more strictly, the two 'love-children', Eliza Williams and Willoughby's illegitimate daughter, for whom the Brandons are responsible, don't 'signify' in this text. Or if they do, they signify through the silence about them. All we know of Margaret is that at thirteen she did not 'bid fair to equal her sisters' (Chapter 1, p. 6). As romantic as the ill-fated Eliza, she calls Willoughby 'Marianne's preserver' (Chapter 10, p. 41), and then virtually disappears from the text. Eliza flickers into the text in Mrs Jennings's sudden memory and in the euphemism of Willoughby's 'connection', but is otherwise the subject of amnesia after Colonel Brandon's revelation to Elinor.

Two sisters make the aesthetic, 'Anglican' settlement Jane Austen habitually arranges for her heroines. This tends to be politically conservative and thus ideologically unworrying. Through taste and talent, sense and sensibility, they win the hearts of men above them in status and/or in wealth. They enter the class of the traditional gentlemanly professions closest to the aristocracy, marrying into the clergy and the army. Marianne, the volatile, dark, unconventional beauty who defies the conventional preference among aestheticians for fair-skinned, definitively European women, marries a rich man in the end. Even the comparatively poor Elinor plans her fashionable sweep in front of the parsonage-house with Edward. So two lively, remarkable girls succeed. Two other 'sisters', to use the filiative language whose meaning is so regularly stretched in the novel, remain. One is a middle-class girl without fortune in the care of a romantic mother. The other is an unclassed girl who, hardly older than Margaret, is a mother herself. The settlement does not include these sisters. The text abounds in detail of piercing sharpness. One of the last pictures we are given of Edward, for instance, is his embarrassment over Lucy's defection, cutting the sheath of a pair of scissors to pieces. No such details are allowed to prefigure the experience of these girls. There is no solution to these ruthless interpretative blanks except amnesia – or interrogation.

One other person is left out of the novel, and that is God. Edward, of course, but only in the Humean sense by remote connection, is His representative, and perhaps this does not bode altogether well. But the fact is that though piety, morality, duty and ethics saturate the text there is no obvious reference to the deity, and, though this is characteristic of Jane Austen, it is unusual for a novel of the time. In this novel

God is a slightly awkward problem; for the sceptic empiricist made Him remote even if the concept of God was retained. Common-sense theory made God axiomatic: Reid wrote, 'We have reason to ascribe to the all-knowing and all-perfect Being distinct conceptions of all things existent and possible, and of all their relations.' For him, God upheld a knowable signifying system. Once one begins to question knowableness, as Jane Austen's novel does, theological certainty is much harder to retain. The move from thinking in terms of Being to Knowing is itself an undermining move away from ontology to epistemology. Perhaps this is why the emphasis on ethics and conduct is called in to redress the distance of God, and why the new discourse of aesthetics is both politicized and moralized, to hold it in place. The new secular, aesthetic and psychological virtues of sense and sensibility are invoked, and pushed towards social meaning to assuage the theological problem. But the absences of God, Margaret and Eliza, a strange trinity, surely reinforce one another.

In the beautiful, assured, 'picturesque' description of Barton Valley, which is both pastiche and innovative visual writing in its own right, reconfiguring the picturesque conventions as it does, an unusual symbolic moment occurs. I have already quoted the description, but end by returning to its concluding lines: 'The hills which surrounded the cottage terminated the valley in that direction; under another name, and in another course, it branched out again between two of the steepest of them' (Chapter 6, p. 25). The pre-determined 'course' or channel of connection which changes its name by the arbitrary imposition of another signification epitomizes the unstable nature of 'connection' in the text. Further, the valley is a feminine symbol, where the woman's body is gently incorporated into the imagery of geology. The image naturalizes the expected progress of feminine experience: 'under another name', the name of a husband; and in another course, in the new channel of marriage; 'It *branched* [emphasis added] out again', it becomes part of, and helps to create, another family 'tree', that ever-recurrent social unit in the text. The lives of both Elinor and Marianne take on these expected contours, but the very artifice of the picturesque cunningly shows how contrived this account is. It is at variance with the absences of the text – God, the *tabula rasa* of Margaret's consciousness, and the only too marked experience of Eliza, who will never take on 'another name'.

A Final Word on the Title: A False Antithesis

Towards the conclusion of this study it is natural to return to the title and to ask what content can finally be given to the words 'Sense' and 'Sensibility'. It is reasonable, perhaps, to expect an overview after the fullness of the narrative has been explored. The impulse to fix meanings and to decide which 'side' Jane Austen was on is powerfully driven by the need for closure. But the immense ambition of this novel, which is in the tradition of the great rationalist eighteenth-century 'Enquiry', and which challenges two key words of its culture, refuses such closure. It demonstrates, indeed, what mobile terms these were. The novel progressively complicates its title words. This should be apparent in my study, which moves from the critique of family as the basis of society, to the 'private', but nevertheless politicized sphere of the aesthetic as a foundation for living, to the psychology of affect, and finally to the ethics and epistemology round the meaning of 'evidence'. I tackle the title obliquely. My four sections move successively from the public to the private and then to the question of feeling, explored largely through Marianne, and finally to the question of judgement and reason, explored largely through Elinor.

What is manifestly clear is that it is not the *antithesis* between sense and sensibility which is being reinforced in the novel. On the contrary, the novel explores the persistent and damaging way in which social structures and subjectivities are *founded* on this split, this polarization, between sense and sensibility, reason and feeling, in Jane Austen's culture. Elinor is not the rational standard from which the emotional Marianne deviates. But it is this model which provides the problem. The education of the emotions is valued. Hysteria, the incipient somatic condition of the novel, does not always arise from too much feeling, but too little, as both Fanny Dashwood's violent outbreak of feeling and the strain of Sir John Middleton's uneasily cheerful benevolence suggest. The only moment at which Willoughby becomes convincing is the time when he begs Marianne, through Elinor, to feel a more 'natural', spontaneous, and less rational forgiveness for him. What kind of society, what kind of subjectivity, emerges if we accept the Humean split, itself an attempt to demonstrate their interaction, between abstraction and sensation, thought and feeling? This is the project of enquiry adopted by the novel and this occasions its deepest unease.

The insistent, overdetermined doubling and opposition in the novel is both a sign of its attempts to escape from the antithetical reading of sense and sensibility and a form of analysis. For Jane Austen both sense and sensibility have become desocialized: they are private, individualist psychological categories which justify a new culture of exploitation, economic and sexual. John Dashwood's entrepreneurial rationalism drives an economic understanding of family. His bourgeois possessive individualism is different in kind from the callousness of Willoughby's affective aristocratic sensibility but similar in its effects.

There is an attempt to give a different content to sense and sensibility and to explore their interdependence by seeing how the terms operate in the alternative 'family' and fragile aesthetic community of intellectual women founded by the Dashwoods. One critic, Deborah Kaplan, in *Jane Austen Among Women* (1992), has suggested that this is the strategy Jane Austen herself adopted to survive, arguing that it confirmed the subordination of women through domestic ideology rather than being an emancipating possibility. However, it is less subordination that troubles the novel than the fact that this aesthetic state does not really *work*. The utopian ideal of a community bonded by sensitivity, reflectiveness and ethical scrupulousness, fusing the vitality implied in the semantic possibilities of both sense and sensibility with judgement and feeling, is entertained. It is a truly civic community in which emotion drives judgement and judgement in its turn drives the aroused hermeneutic desires of the picturesque. Shared critique and interpretative activity is possible here. But the possibility for critique implied in the picturesque also explodes this self-contained civil society or 'aesthetic state'. The aesthetic cannot exist outside other social forms and practices, nor can it assuage the cruelty of these forms. Not only does the external world constantly invade it but the category of the aesthetic is shown not to transcend politics. It participates in the very conditions of power it seeks to evade. As tasteful sense it can be authoritarian in its need to order, and the need to order becomes a form of efficient economic management. As affective aristocratic culture of the feelings through sensibility it can be brutal. The aristocratic and bourgeois reading of sensibility complicates matters. The critical vision opened up by the gaps and lacunae of the picturesque is quite different from the commanding power of the overview envisaged by the aristocratic picturesque. The critical picturesque can produce an individualist, self-referring sensibility or the interrogative sensibility of the shared critique. In the context of the aesthetic, sense and sensibility take on more mobile meanings than anywhere in the novel. The contradictory political meanings of sensibility in particular, that which nurtures aristocratic forms, and that which produces radical passion, are constantly present in this context. The novel clings to an ideal of the aesthetic while knowing that it can belong to the will for power.

Sense and Sensibility spans the period over which, as Gary Kelly puts it in his *Women, Writing and Revolution* (1993), there was a 'remasculinization' of culture, and in many ways the novel is one of the last attempts to see what place there is for a 'feminine' reading of the possibility of a consciousness where an interdependent judgement and sensibility co-exist. But perhaps most remarkable is the novel's celebration of vitality despite the darkness of its social vision. The root meanings Johnson draws from both sense and sensibility, suggesting alertness to the sensory, are never far away from the novel. This, perhaps, grounds social experience because a response to the sensory, even if we cannot get into one another's bodies, is what is held in common, what everyone can read. The novel uses the energy of the interrogative techniques of sensibility and the physicality of the picturesque to expose the libertine, prostitute and colonial adventurer who underpin both aristocratic and bourgeois subjectivity. It shows, through its vigorous response to the complexity of sense data, that the only *rational* order is one which is repeatedly consensually revised because there is no intrinsic rational coherence to experience except the one we impose ourselves. This points back again to Johnson's understanding of sense as coherence rather than order. Repeatedly sense and sensibility are pushed away from their psychological meanings and towards a semantic network of both physical and social significations, which gives them vivacity and strength. Reasoning which recognizes neither the intense somatic nature of experience nor the collaborative nature of judgement hollows out the self. Hubristically Cartesian or inhibited and passive, such a form of reason thins out the consciousness. By the same token, feeling which is divorced from an interactive social world is abstract and solipsist, opening the way for economic and emotional exploitation, whether it exploits or is exploited. Neither attribute on its own is capable of giving rise to the analysis the subject needs to survive as a fully social – and sexual – human being. Conceived of alone as single principles of existence they pathologize. The words of its title threaten to destabilize the novel so complex do they become, as 'good' and 'bad' meanings of both words struggle in the text. On the other hand, in the disturbingly ungrounded world of *Sense and Sensibility*, hysteria and melancholia, sensibility and sense respectively gone morbid, threaten to prevail unless we can hang on to the possibility that its abstract nouns can have a meaningful cultural value.

Conclusion: The Jane Austen Debate

The ungrounded nature of *Sense and Sensibility* – a deliberate strategy in my view, suggesting the ungroundedness of Jane Austen's society – makes it difficult to be categorical about anything in it. For instance, Jane Austen did not appear to like *Hamlet* very much, to judge by her letters. In the year *Sense and Sensibility* was published she wrote of the 'unlucky change' by which a performance of *King John* in London was replaced with *Hamlet* (18 April 1811).[1] She went to see something else instead. And yet, whether she liked the play or not, that play seems to be a constant presence in her novel. Of course, except by a reading of the text I can't prove this, particularly as there are no direct quotations from *Hamlet* in the novel, and even then, someone might wish to invoke the letter to close discussion. All I can assert is that the novel begins to 'signify', as Mrs Jennings would say, when *Hamlet* is invoked.

When it comes to arguing about the ideological meaning of Jane Austen's texts, the position is the same. It is not easy to be categorical about her politics. Modern Jane Austen criticism has largely rejected George Moore's disparaging view of her 'maiden lady realism': 'I know nothing of the natural sciences, of politics, of metaphysics, nor have I attempted to plumb the depths of the human soul; I am a maiden lady, interested in the few people with whom my lot is cast. If you care to know how So-and-so married So-and-so I will tell you.' Since Marilyn Butler's *Jane Austen and the War of Ideas* (1975, rev. 1987), which initiated a new historical and political reading of Jane Austen, and an intense debate about her politics (a debate which has begun to weary some people), it has been impossible to read as naively as Moore, for though the surface of the texts are deceptively 'historyless', it is clear that this is far from the case. Marilyn Butler argues for a conservative, anti-Jacobin Jane Austen. In addition, she believes that the feminist debates of the late seventies, and eighties at least, are not relevant to Austen. Her book is still central to Austen criticism.

She has been answered by Claudia L. Johnson, in *Jane Austen: Women, Politics and the Novel* (1988). The situation is a complex one because political debates are crossed with debates within feminism. Let us start with the politics and move to the sexual politics explored in criticism of Jane Austen's work, though both, of course, are involved with one another.

Claudia Johnson argues less that Jane Austen is 'subversive', the argument which most irritates Marilyn Butler, than that she was 'sceptical about reactionary ideology' (19) and that the critique of conservative ideology, both of the family and of sensibility (which she takes to be a mode of 'feminine' conformism) is 'trenchant' (69). Indeed, she sees *Sense and Sensibility* as the most progressive of the novels in its social criticism. Using the poles of conservative and radical fiction by women – the fiction of the counter-revolutionary Elizabeth Hamilton as opposed to the radical Amelia Opie, for instance – as a way of assessing Jane Austen's political position, she demonstrates convincingly that Jane Austen's work does not have a conservative agenda, and that her work can be located in a progressive, though not radical, tradition. It may well be the iconoclastic tradition, which the independent English gentry evolved over the eighteenth century, a radical tradition, actually, which, Marilyn Butler has shown, became alarmed when Jacobinism showed it what these ideas looked like outside the elite. In a study appearing in the same year as Johnson's, however, *Between Self and World: The Novels of Jane Austen* (1988), James Thompson argues that Jane Austen's critique always dissolved ideology into morality and that she never really questioned the structures of her society. On the other hand, another 'progressive' reading occurs in Oliver MacDonagh's *Jane Austen: Real and Imagined Worlds* (1991), which matches up the facts of the novels against the facts of Jane Austen's life, and finds that in *Sense and Sensibility* 'money constitutes a sort of underlying beat below the narrative', from the conspicuous consumption of Robert Ferrar's jewelled toothpick case to the indigence of the Dashwoods. He notices 'a most striking correspondence between the widowed Mrs Dashwood's situation as an almost rent-free tenant of Barton Cottage with three daughters, two maidservants and a man, on a joint income of £500 a year, and the widowed Mrs Austen's as the rent-free tenant of Chawton with two daughters and one quasi-daughter, two maidservants and a man, and a joint income of £500 a year' (63). A rather different reading, tending to the conservative paradigm, is Myra Stokes's fastidious and very useful *The Language of Jane Austen: A Study of Some Aspects of Her Vocabulary* (1991), where the semantic fields of key words as they would have been understood in Jane Austen's time are mapped out. 'Taste' (173) and the 'Picturesque' (181–3) are helpfully glossed.

The ding-dong of conservative/non-conservative argument seems to proliferate indefinitely. I have discussed the problem of Jane Austen's politics elsewhere (in the Penguin Critical Studies series volume on

Mansfield Park). I argued that the Jane Austen text is mobile – the volatility of the word 'sensibility', with both its Burkean and radical meanings, is a case in point. The Jane Austen text permits, encourages, critique, and opens up a space for a radical reading. Whatever officially held beliefs Jane Austen might have professed (and how can we really determine them except through the text?), the text in its volatility cannot confirm these. The Jane Austen text is not the kind that goes for a single-minded Anglican-conservative agenda. To accept this would be to think of her texts as if they were the ideologically closed writings of a novelist such as Charlotte Yonge (another Anglican conservative) – and they are patently not.

But a little more needs to be said. First, Jane Austen's texts could be read from a number of subject positions, not only in our own day but when they were produced. That's part of the narrative pleasure and part of the point of having an Elinor and a Marianne. At times she can even provide the metaphysical comfort which Nietszche thought of as the need of the new consumerist (and in his sense reactionary) middle class. At times she refuses this pleasure. How 'subversive' the Jane Austen text is may be open to question, but it allows different groups and subgroups in Jane Austen's time (from conservative to radical, upper-middle class, rising-middle class) to take up different reading positions in a way which other texts do not. And this involves taking up not only one's 'own' reading position but being made aware of the possibility of others. We do not have to read obstinately against the grain in order to accept this. Lucy Steele's social ambitions demand recognition, for instance, and so does Elinor's rational conservatism.

This is not just because the novels are open-endedly complex, or because they fall across 'faultlines' in their culture, a concept explored in other contexts by the cultural materialist, Alan Sinfield.[2] The idea of the faultline in ideology, using geology as a metaphor to suggest the involuntarily (and inevitably) fissured text, suggests that the rifted text springs a weakness of which the writer is hardly aware; indeed, he or she cannot be aware of the faultline because it is produced by virtue of the very attempt to produce ideological closure and is constituted by the pressure which builds up through the act of closure and its strain. The faultline may provide a welcome release of tension, and allow *other* people to see the strains and contradictions of the text. But it is never something that can be negotiated by the text. This looks oddly as if cultural materialism is smuggling the unconscious in under the guise of a geological metaphor, a kind of ideological unconscious. It means that there is a certain arbitrariness about how we decide what is known and not known by the text. Such 'cultural historicism' differs only from other more straightforward political readings in that it assumes we can understand what the *fixed* positions of the text are, but unlike them it goes on to determine the repressed readings which can then be disclosed.

But in a complex text can we ever determine unambiguously what these 'fixed' positions may be? If we think of the text as an enquiry, an exploration, such a model defies fixity. It permits anxiety, mobility, revision, ambivalence – and ambivalence about ambivalence. It also allows us to think of a text in which the writer struggles to take the text's problems into her own hands and to negotiate them actively rather than being oblivious to its own faultlines. Throughout this book I have spoken sometimes of 'Jane Austen' and sometimes of 'the text' to indicate this volatile struggle with meaning in which sometimes the author and sometimes her material gains ascendancy. I emphasize this point because some of the new historicist readings which have begun to emerge in studies in Romanticism sometimes look oddly like the old historical readings where fixity is at a premium. True, there are problems with a new historicism which textualizes history as well as historicizing the text, but it is not easy, either, to make an appeal to a fixed history as a prior authority. James Thompson reminds his readers of Raymond Williams's warnings against 'the reduction of the social to fixed forms' (130). And in Jane Austen's case there is a tendency to assume there is only one kind of history to discover. David Monaghan, for instance, in his *Jane Austen: Structure and Social Vision* (1980), quotes Burke, 'the great philosopher of the landed interest', as if his views can be transferred unproblematically into the novels:

To be attached to the subdivision, to love the little platoon we belong to in society, is the first principle (the germ as it were) of Public affections. It is the first link in the series by which we proceed to love of our country and to mankind.

The strategy here is to credit Jane Austen hypothetically with Burke's ideology before reading the text and then to proceed to discover it there. Something of the same kind worries Roger Gard in his *Jane Austen's Novels: The Art of Clarity* (1992) when, in his introductory chapter, he considers Marilyn Butler's insistence on a return to the codes of Anglican conservatism governing Jane Austen's narrative. But his solution, to let slip the knot of history, is unnecessarily extreme. History can never be abandoned: but the mobility of the text and the nature of history as representation with its own form of fictionality must surely not be abandoned either. The real problem is not to get 'back' to history, perhaps, but to find a way of holding mobile political ideas and literary form together.

Feminist readings of Jane Austen tend to discover either rebellion or orthodoxy among her protagonists, concentrating on the enforced passivity prompted by the ideological work of gender, and almost exclusively on the *subjectivity* of particular characters in order to argue for the repression of the feminine subject. Marianne is almost always seen as a victim. Sandra Gilbert and Susan Gubar's *Madwoman in the Attic* (1979) and Mary Poovey's *The Proper Lady* (1984) are frequently quoted in support of this kind of feminist analysis, where women cede control of their identities. Deborah Kaplan's *Jane Austen Among Women* (1992) suggests that in accepting a separate sphere Jane Austen colluded with male power rather than releasing herself from it. But there are actually very different kinds of feminist reading available to feminist analysis. Mary Evans's *Jane Austen and the State* (1987), for instance, examines structures rather than subjectivities (Willoughby for her is capitalist man and his exploitative individualism). One of the earliest feminist readings, by Margaret Kirkham, reminded readers of the enlightenment feminism which asserted that women shared the same moral natures as men and argued that Jane Austen subscribed to this position.

The feminist debate is riven. People tend to assume that a feminist reading signals a progressive text and that a progressive text signals feminist openings. But this is actually far from the case. Arguably many feminist readings offer a highly restricted account of Jane Austen's texts. Julia Prewitt Brown has complained about what she sees as these betrayals by middle-class feminism in a vigorous review article of 1989 in *Novel* (23, 303–13). She attacks feminist readings for their subjectivist premises and 'self-laceration and self-pity' (304), for their unhistorical insistence on the oppressive social order of Austen's time (Gilbert and Gubar, Poovey), and for a narrow reading of the political simply in terms of left and right (Johnson), which, she thinks, a genuinely political reading can transcend. But how? And though she insists on a return to the philosphical traditions of Wollstonecraftian feminism, it is hard to see how this radicalism can belong at the same time to the Lockean tradition which she feels Jane Austen belongs to, at least as it was taken up in the enlightenment. Many of her arguments are telling. She is right to see Jane Austen exploring cultural shifts, but her own politics seem to go out of focus from time to time despite the sharpness of her perceptions.

Interestingly, her arguments are solely with American feminists, which makes one aware of the very different traditions of American feminism in comparison with those of European feminism. American feminism's concern with woman's oppression through confinement to the domestic sphere, on passivity and on the recuperation of a feminine tradition, is not echoed to the same extent in British studies. This is not the place to explore the phenomenon further, but it may be that the very different conditions of American culture have led American feminists to read Jane Austen's texts through the place of women in the American puritan tradition, whereas the history of European women has been different. Nevertheless, despite the formulations which have with some justice irritated Marilyn Butler, the influx of American feminism has been wholly good for a tradition which emphasized Jane Austen's 'maiden lady realism' for too long. American feminism has galvanized Jane Austen studies, and forced them to entertain questions of gender as well as seeking intellectual traditions in which to see her work. To subtract this influence would leave us with a less exciting and important debate.

Probably the most notorious and challenging contribution to the Jane Austen debate is Eve Kosovsky Sedgwick's 'Jane Austen and the Masturbating Girl', in *Critical Inquiry* (17, 1990–91, 818–37). It deliberately sweeps aside the insistent moralizing of Jane Austen's work and the polarization of Elinor and Marianne. The puritan tradition here calls forth its transgressive other with a vengeance the writer exuberantly enjoys. Sedgwick shows how the language describing Marianne's excessive grief has affinities with a late-nineteenth century pornographic text on female masturbation. She is forced to control herself but cannot, and the more insistent the control, the more intense and outrageous the impulse. Elinor's consent to repression hollows out her subjectivity. A Foucauldian essay, it is concerned with the text's compulsion to circulate a hidden discourse. The more forbidden, the more it erupts into the text. It is an allegory of both the reader's and the critic's compulsion. We too resort 'again and again' (Chapter 1, p. 6) to those taboo experiences in which we work upon ourselves. Any reply to this essay looks stuffy – it very skilfully blocks off a response. My own sense is that the intense mourning of *Sense and Sensibility* precludes the jouissance, forbidden or not, which is being described. But this article was intended to be a must for the critic and clearly is so, as an important account of the formation of nineteenth-century subjectivity.

Confronted with so much disagreement, is it possible to say what kind of writer Jane Austen was? I believe it is possible to elicit some propositions from the mobile enquiry of her texts. I believe her to be a profound writer and a passionate one. Consequently I find her comments about herself as a miniaturist working in ivory slightly irritating. She seems to have been able to sense, explore, challenge and make problematical the central, controversial philosophical values and political ideas of her culture and to understand how it formed subjectivity. Her novels debate daringly with other texts and within themselves. How far she knew well any of the works I have mentioned is open to question. To such queries about the ground of this intertextuality I have to return the same Mrs Jennings answer, that these texts 'signify' when invoked. It must be remembered that Jane Austen is a comic writer, and in the seriousness of my response to her comedy I may seem to have forgotten this, but I will make up for this heavy-handedness by remembering it now. Her novels are saturated in sexual feeling in an almost brazen way. Her understanding of social forms and class is scandalously knowing as well as subtle. She has the social climber's hypersensitivity and the fastidiousness of the person for whom learning is knowledge as well as power. Her language is seeringly precise – or if it is not precise its ambiguities are not fudged, but open up searching interpretative questions.

Given this – though perhaps not everyone would accept my account – one would expect her texts to be ideologically complex. She was the daughter of a relatively poor Anglican clergyman who worked tirelessly (and successfully) for the advancement of his sons and clung to the coat-tails of the landed gentry. The formation she belonged to by birth and probably by conviction was Anglican conservative and anti-Jacobin. Yet her social position was tenuous, particularly because it was occupied by a woman living without the protection of marriage. This would be likely to make someone either want to reaffirm conservative values as a way of consolidating a sense of social identity, or, as a perilously just-not-outsider, to be horribly aware of the social violence with which all hierarchies are constructed. Any reasonably complex subject would be likely to experience both awarenesses at once. There is no reason why we should assume the eighteenth/nineteenth-century subject to be less complicated than ourselves: different, to be sure, but not less complicated. Therefore, since one can extrapolate these contradictory positions from the biography, I am not sure that it helps to rest on one rather than the other in interpreting the novels. Jane Austen's texts actively negotiate with their culture. I don't believe that Austen seriously wanted to see liberté, egalité and fraternité in her society, but the pressures of these ideologies are never far from her work. She took them on, in a way lesser novelists do not. On the other hand I do not think, either, that the 'aesthetic Anglican' settlements with which the novels end really matter very much in comparison with the extraordinarily strenuous and precise critique going on in the body of the novels.

Her women characters are the key, because they are people who are genuinely liberated from the conventional mores of the conduct books. She was fascinated by authority and the regulation of desire, and on how you ground life in that contradiction in terms, a sceptical teleology. In *Sense and Sensibility* deregulation is allowed to let rip through the absence of the father – sexually (Willoughby), aesthetically (Marianne), financially (the John Dashwoods) – in order to see what happens to people in this kind of society and in order to see what happens to society itself when it lacks this ground. She made an out-and-out critique of the exploitative mercantilism which was redefining and commodifying family 'connections' while respecting its energies (Mrs Jennings) and even its opportunism. Women without money are a test case because they raise the question how far it is possible to live in this society. And she manages to make living, palpitating experience out of their dilemmas. There are few models of successful communality in her work. She was sceptical of bogus Tory claims on tradition and hierarchy, and of the phoney erasure of class through the levelling of sentimental benevolence. I find it very difficult to know whether or not some of her characters are allegories of dangerous, unbound Jacobin rebelliousness, partly because she loved energy, and partly because so many of the novels were revised over so many years, and the political ground had shifted between the 1790s and the first decade of the nineteenth century. Violence and then the answer it called forth, repression, were successively threats to the state over the years Jane Austen was writing.

What Jane Austen never gave up was the right of critique. And because this goes deep, emancipatory moments flash out in her work. These are important, but not continuous, as her critical analysis is. Her *analysis* is always of political significance even when her specific political allegiance is in question. She pulled out metaphysical comfort from under the feet of the middle class almost brutally at times. That is why I name her as a disturbing, undermining, challenging figure. The original military meaning of 'subvert', to raze a city to the ground, is not one readily associated with her work. But, though she clearly believed in their importance, she held the arrangements of civil society up to scrutiny remorselessly. And moreover she did this with what Walter Benjamin described as the supreme qualities of the storyteller's art of resistance – cunning and high spirits.

Notes

The edition quoted from is *Sense and Sensibility* (1811), Ros Ballaster ed., Harmondsworth (Penguin Classics), 1995.

Introduction and Section One

1. Samuel Johnson, *A Dictionary of the English Language*, 3 vols, London, 1755.
2. The following explore the literary and cultural significance of 'Sensibility' and new accounts of subjectivity: John Mullan, *Sentiment and Sociability: The Language of Feeling in the Eighteenth Century*, Oxford, 1988; *Technologies of the Self: A Seminar with Michel Foucault*, Luther H. Martin et al., eds, Amherst, Mass., 1988; dealing with a slightly later period but relevant to the debate, see Regenia Gagnier, *Subjectivities: A History of Self-Representation in Britain. 1832–1920*, New York, 1991. See also John Dwyer, *Virtuous Discourse: Sensibility and Community in late Eighteenth-Century Scotland*, Edinburgh, 1987. An introductory survey is Janet Todd, *Sensibility: An Introduction*, London and New York, 1986.
3. Mary Wollstonecraft, *Vindication of the Rights of Woman* (1792), Miriam Kramnick, ed., Harmondsworth, 1975 (repr. 1982), 130.
4. See the brilliant discussion of the words 'Sense and Sensibility' and the remarks on Austen's novel in William Empson, *The Structure of Complex Words*, London, 1951, 250–69. See also, Ernest Gellner, *Reason and Culture: The Historic Role of Reason and Rationalism*, Oxford, 1992, 1–29; 136–9; for a discussion of Cartesian reason in enlightenment thought and culture.
5. Margaret Anne Doody (following Chesterton), who sees Jane Austen's earlier work as a spirited critique of orthodoxy, in her edition of *Catharine and Other Writings* (World's Classics), Oxford and New York, 1993. Subsequent quotations from *Love and Freindship* are taken from this edition. Margaret Doody has also edited *Sense and Sensibility* in the Oxford World's Classics edition (1990) with a challenging introduction emphasizing Austen's intelligence and sophistication.
6. The social origins and financial circumstances of the Austens are discussed by Park Honan, *Jane Austen: A Life*, London, 1887, 11–20.
7. Ida Macalpine and Richard Hunter, *George III and the Mad-Business*, London, 1969, 14–46; 111–42. Recurrent bouts of insanity, or what was interpreted as insanity, occurred in 1788, 1801, 1804, before the Regency Act of 1811.
8. Marilyn Butler, *Jane Austen and the War of Ideas* (1975), rev. edn, with new Introduction, Oxford, 1987. Her subsequent *Romantics, Rebels and Reactionaries: English Literature and its Background 1760–1830*, Oxford and New York, 1981, gives a further context for literary responses to Jacobinism and counter-revolutionary movements.
9. For an account of counter-revolutionary reaction see H. T. Dickinson,

129

British Radicalism and the French Revolution, Oxford and New York, 1985 (repr. 1988), 25–42. Dickinson makes careful reservations both about the *unity* of radicalism and about the strength of reaction.

10. Butler, *Jane Austen and the War of Ideas*, 182–96. Marilyn Butler sees Marianne as the representative of dangerous, antisocial and revolutionary Rousseauian feeling, 'individualism, or the worship of self' (194). It would be just as easy to see her as the thoughtless ally of Whig aristocratic consumerism, using landscape for her own emotional purposes. The politics of women's writing and the complexity of the positions that could be taken up in the period are explored in a study of two radicals and one conservative woman writer by Gary Kelly, *Women, Writing, and Revolution*, Oxford, 1993. The contemporary debate about Jane Austen and politics in the Romantic period, which is crossed by feminist debates (themselves fractured with ideological disagreement) and debates about the meaning of the feminine at this period, intensified in the late 1980s as the concepts and practices of new historicism entered studies in Romanticism. Marilyn Butler's argument for a conservative Jane Austen has been challenged by Claudia L. Johnson, *Jane Austen, Women, Politics and the Novel*, Chicago, 1988. Julia Prewitt Brown, an early contributor (1979) to the debate on Jane Austen's response to the social order, has in turn criticized Johnson for a narrow feminism in a review essay in *Novel*, 23, 1989, 303–13. A balanced and highly discriminating account of Jane Austen's politics is made by Gene W. Ruoff, *Jane Austen's Sense and Sensibility*, Hemel Hempstead, 1992.

11. See Clive Emsley, *British Society and the French Wars 1793–1815*, London, 1979. E. J. Hobsbawm's overview, particularly his section, 'War', *The Age of Revolution 1789–1848*, London, 1962 (reprinted 1992), 101–25, can be supplemented by John Ramsden, 'The struggle against France 1793–1815' (Chapter 9), *Ruling Britannia: A Political History of Britain 1688–1988*, Glyn Williams, John Ramsden, eds, London and New York, 1990, 152–71.

12. James M. Holzman, *Nabobs in England: A Study of the Returned Anglo Indian 1760–1785*, New York, 1926, 17, 40. Pitt's India Act in 1784 modified the powers of the East India Company to some extent, but Clive's policy of virtual extortion for protection enriched great numbers of East India officers. Returning Nabobs were ostracized despite their wealth, and women would refuse to dance with them (19). Holzman describes the Nabob thus: 'The Nabob was, in general, a civil or military servant of the Company, who enriched himself by exploiting the advantages which the establishment of British political dominion in India gave to the officials of the ruling power on the spot' (8). For the English in India rather than the Nabob at home see also Percival Spear, *The Nabobs: A Study of the Social Life of the English in Eighteenth-Century India*, rev. edn, London, 1963.

13. Anna Laetitia Barbauld, *Eighteen Hundred and Eleven, A Poem*, London, 1812, 1–2; 3–4; 5.

14. See Neil McKendrick, John Brewer, J. H. Plumb, *The Birth of a Consumer Society: The Commercialisation of Eighteenth-Century England*, London, 1982.

15. 'Her behaviour is pathological in a way which for the late-eighteenth century could have been construed as madness': Tony Tanner (ed.) *Sense and Sensibility*, Harmondsworth, 1969, 8. This is one of the finest introductions to the novel.

16. See, on heirship strategies, Lawrence Stone, Jeanne C. Fawtier Stone, *An Open Elite? England 1540–1880*, Oxford, 1984, 120. See also James Casey, *The History of the Family*, Oxford, 1989.

17. For records of the 'adoption', see George Holbert Tucker, *A Goodly Heritage: A History of Jane Austen's Family*, Manchester, 1983.

18. Stone, *An Open Elite?*, 283.

19. For the economic and social significance of transport, see G. R. Hawke, J. P. P. Higgins, 'Transport and social overhead capital', *The Economic History of Britain Since 1700*, Roderick Floud, Donald McCloskey, eds, 2 vols, Cambridge, 1981, I (1700–1860), 227–51.

20. Stone, *An Open Elite?*, 282–4; 421. See also Alistair M. Duckworth, *The Improvement of the Estate: A Study of Jane Austen's Novels*, Baltimore, 1971.

21. Stone, *An Open Elite?*, 412–14.

22. There is a useful discussion of 'connexions' (*sic*) and their relation to 'interests' in Asa Briggs, *The Age of Improvement*, London, New York, Toronto, 1959, 106–8.

Section Two

1. See, for an account of the Bluestocking Circle, Sylvia Harcstark Myers, *The Bluestocking Circle: Women, Friendship, and the Life of the Mind in Eighteenth-Century England*, Oxford, 1990. Also, for the Bluestockings' problematical relations to family, see Gary Kelly, *Women, Writing, and Revolution 1790–1827*, Oxford, 1993, 150–51.

2. *Columella, or the Distressed Anchoret* (1776), 2 vols, London, 1779, II, 66. Richard Graves also satirizes a number of contemporary affectations including picturesque landscape. The toothpick case ordered by Robert Ferrars might derive from Graves's attack on affluence (II, 245).

3. Goldsmith's *The Deserted Village* (1770), idealizes rural life and laments the depopulation of the rural village. Crabbe's *The Village* (1783) is an anti-pastoral poem attacking the idyll of country life and work described by Goldsmith. For the representation of the rural in England see *The English Rural Community: Image and Analysis*, Brian Short, ed., Cambridge, 1992.

4. Robert Southey, *Sir Thomas More: or Colloquies*, 2 vols, London, 1829, I, 174. Thomas Macaulay replied in a review of 1830, reprinted in *Works of Thomas Macaulay*, London, 1897, V, 342.

5. *The Poetical Works of Wordsworth* (1904, Oxford Standard Authors), Ernest De Selincourt, ed., rev. edn, London, New York and Toronto, 1950, 599.

6. *Columella*, II, 77; 229.

7. William Gilpin, *Observations on the Western Parts of England*, London, 1798, 255.

8. Gilpin, *Observations on the Western Parts of England*, 328.

9. Gilpin, *Observations on the River Wye*, London, 1770, 14.

10. John Barrell, *The Idea of Landscape and the Sense of Place 1730–1840: An Approach to the Poetry of John Clare*, London, 1972. Barrell argues throughout that the picturesque is the aesthetic of ownership, where the eye is at 'ease in landscape which had been enclosed' (32), that is, in landscape which betokens uninterrupted ownership of the land viewed.

11. *The Poetical Works of William Cowper* (1905, Oxford Standard Authors), H. S. Milford, ed., 4th edn, London, New York and Toronto, 1934, 135.

12. *The Poems of James Thomson* (1908, Oxford Standard Authors), J. Logie Robertson, ed., London, New York and Toronto, repr. 1961, 144.

13. The bourgeois criteria of efficiency and land management is typified in Arthur Young, whose tours of England in the 1770s are those of the professionalized agriculturalist, a drive to efficiency encouraged by the French wars and the setting up of a semi-official Board of Agriculture in 1793. See Arthur Young, *Rural Oeconomy, or Essays on the Practical Parts of Husbandry*, Dublin, 1770. Young believed that maximizing profit depended on good 'management' (13) which encouraged 'proportion' (7) between various functions of the land. In *The Rural Socrates* he stated that a meritocratic republic encouraged the aspirations of labourers (2nd edn, 1764, 310). Later he wrote in an anti-Jacobin vein.

14. Uvedale Price, *A Dialogue on the Distinct Characters of the Picturesque and the Beautiful*, London, 1801, 112; 160. Price's *Essays on the Picturesque* appeared 1794–8 (though I feel his ideas are theorized more strenuously in the later work), and so this aesthetic would have been known to Jane Austen when she returned to her novel.

15. Walter John Hipple, *The Beautiful, the Sublime and the Picturesque in Eighteenth-century British Aesthetic Theory*, Carbondale, 1957, 241, summarizes the political argument in which Price disagreed with Repton on establishing a 'mean' in landscape on analogy with the British constitution. He celebrated 'freedom, energy, and variety' in a national character unfit for 'thraldom'.

16. Price, *Dialogue*, 28.

17. Price, *Dialogue*, 102.

18. *Windsor Forest* (1713), 31–2; 42. *The Poems of Alexander Pope*, John Butt, ed., 6 vols, London and New Haven, 1953–67, 1, 1961.

19. Marilyn Butler, *Jane Austen and the War of Ideas* (1975), rev. edn, Oxford, 1987, 194.

20. Gilpin, *Observations on the Western Parts of England*, 328; 175.

21. Richard Payne Knight, *An Analytical Enquiry into the Principles of Taste*, London, 1805, 50.

22. Hannah More, *Essays on Various Subjects. Principally Designed for Young Ladies*, London, 1777, 145. 'That bold, independent, enterprising spirit, which is so much admired in boys, should not, when it happens to discover itself in the other sex, be encouraged, but suppressed' (145).

23. John Gregory, *A Father's Legacy to his Daughters* (1774), quoted in Vivien Jones, ed., *Women in the Eighteenth Century*, London, 1990, 45.

24. Edmund Burke, *A Philosophical Enquiry into the Origin of Our Ideas of the Sublime and Beautiful* (1757), Adam Phillips, ed. (World's Classics), Oxford and New York, 1990, Part III, Section XVIII, 107.

Section Three

1. Quoted by Vivien Jones, ed., *Women in the Eighteenth Century*, London, 1990, 86.

2. Mary Wollstonecraft, *Vindication of the Rights of Woman* (1792), Miriam Brody Kramnick, ed., Harmondsworth, 1975, 152. For conduct books and

the regulation of sexuality see Jones, N. 1 above: 'Conduct', 14–56; 'Sexuality', 57–97.

3. Richard Payne Knight, *An Analytical Enquiry into the Principles of Taste*, London, 1805, 131; 135.
4. Janet Todd, *Sensibility: An Introduction*, London, 130; for the attack on Sensibility see 129–46.
5. Henry Mackenzie (1745–1831), an Edinburgh lawyer and man of letters, and the author of a number of novels and a play, *The Prince of Tunis* (1773), abridged Cobbett's *Life of Thomas Paine* in 1796. His *The Man of Feeling* has become increasingly important in political readings of sensibility in recent re-readings of eighteenth-century literature. See Robert Markley, 'Sentimentality as Performance: Shaftesbury, Sterne, and the Theatrics of Virtue', in *The New Eighteenth Century: Theory, Politics, English Literature*, Felicity Nussbaum and Laura Brown, eds, New York and London, 1987, 210–30.
6. The edition of *The Man of Feeling* (1771) used is Vol. 29 (1810) of Anna Laetitia Aikin's (Barbauld) *British Novelists*, London, 27. Barbauld's radical connections suggest the context in which Mackenzie was read. See also Brian Vickers, ed., *The Man of Feeling*, London, 1967, vii–xxiv.
7. See above, Section I, N. 12. The discussion on the relative nature of the 'competence' takes place in the context of an attack on the immense fortunes of the Nabob in Graves's *Columella*, II, 229.
8. Mary Poovey, *The Proper Lady and the Woman Writer: Ideology as Style in the Work of Mary Wollstonecraft, Mary Shelley and Jane Austen*, Chicago, 1984, 83–194, argues that Austen oversees an appropriation of women's sexuality by male figures. A number of American feminists have created a tradition of criticism in which the woman writer (and as surrogate her heroines) either achieves a heroic autonomy, liberating herself into her 'own' experience, or suffers the ideological work of oppression to take its course and ceases to challenge her confinement to the domestic and the control of her sexuality. See Ellen Moers, *Literary Women*, London 1977. Elaine Showalter, *A Literature of Their Own*, Princeton, 1977; Sandra Gilbert, Susan Gubar, *Madwoman in the Attic*, New Haven, 1979; Nancy Armstrong, *Desire and Domestic Fiction: A Political History of the Novel*, New York and Oxford, 1987. This work was and is of immense importance, initiating a new wave of feminist discussion and ensuring the continued recognition of gender as a category in criticism. But it tends to exaggerate the lack of autonomy experienced by the woman writer of this period, who could claim professional status and public recognition in her culture.

Section Four

1. See Robert Young, *Torn Halves*, London, 1994. See 'Herder and Organic Culture', chapter II.
2. Working-class and middle-class access to news and knowledge differed because middle-class readers could afford the cost of stamped newspapers. Opinions vary about the success and extent of repressive measures, but there is no doubt that a culture of secrecy was a fact of life for all classes. See Patricia Hollis, *The Pauper Press*, Oxford, 1970.
3. Robert Markley (see above, Section 3, N. 5), quotes (218) from one of Steele's ambivalent discussions of the priorities of merit rather than inheritance in *The*

Guardian, 18 August 1713, 137: Steele questions whether 'a *new* Man of an elevated Merit is not more to be honoured than an insignificant and worthless Man who is descended from a long Line of Patriots and Heroes'.

4. Richard Payne Knight, *An Analytical Inquiry into the Principles of Taste*, London, 1805, 236.
5. Anthony Ashley Cooper, Third Earl of Shaftesbury, *Characteristics of Men, Manners, Opinions and Times*, 3 vols, London, 1711, 2, 112.
6. Adam Smith, *The Theory of Moral Sentiments* (1759), Dugald Stewart, ed., London, 1853, 4. For further discussion of issues of the body see John Wiltshire, *Jane Austen and the Body: 'The Picture of Health'*, Cambridge, 1992.
7. Thomas Reid, *Essay on the Intellectual Powers of Man* (1785), in *British Empirical Philosophers: Locke, Berkely, Hume, Reid and J. S. Mill*, A. J. Ayer and Raymond Winch, eds, London, 1952, 541.
8. Reid, *Essay on the Intellectual Powers of Man*, 520–21.
9. David Hume, *An Enquiry Concerning Human Understanding* (1748), Eric Steinberg, ed., Indianapolis, 1977, 105.
10. David Hume, *A Treatise of Human Nature* (1739), L. A. Selby Bigge, ed., Oxford (1888), repr. 1951, Book III, Part III, Section III, 603.
11. Hume, *Treatise*, Book I, Part I, Section IV, 11.
12. Terry Eagleton argues that Hume, having abandoned 'a sure standard in anything', became fully conscious of 'the fictional nature of the bourgeois economy': *The Ideology of the Aesthetic*, Oxford, 1990, 50.

Conclusion

1. *Jane Austen's Letters to Her Sister Cassandra and Others*, R. W. Chapman, ed., 2nd edn, London and New York, 1952, 18 April 1811, 271.
2. Alan Sinfield, *Faultlines: Cultural Materialism and the Politics of Dissident Reading*, Oxford, 1992.

Bibliography

EDITIONS AND RESEARCH MATERIALS

References are to Ros Ballaster's edition of *Sense and Sensibility*, Harmondsworth (Penguin Classics), 1995. The authoritative edition is R. W. Chapman, *The Novels of Jane Austen*, 5 vols, London, 1932–4, I, *Sense and Sensibility*, 3rd edn, London and New York, 1933. Chapman has also edited *Jane Austen's Letters to Her Sister Cassandra and Others*, 2nd edn, London and New York, 1952. See also *Jane Austen: A Family Record* (1913), William Austen-Leigh and Richard Arthur Austen-Leigh, rev. and enlarged Deidre Le Faye, London (British Library), 1989. George Holbert Tucker, *A Goodly Heritage: A History of Jane Austen's Family*, Manchester, 1983.

STUDIES OF JANE AUSTEN AND HER WORK

B. C. Southam's *Jane Austen: The Critical Heritage*, 2 vols, London, 1968, 1987, collects criticism of Jane Austen by major figures up to 1938. The Book List which follows begins in 1975, the year in which a new debate about Jane Austen, history and politics was initiated.

Marilyn Butler, *Jane Austen and the War of Ideas*, Oxford, 1975, reprinted with new Introduction, 1987.

Barbara Hardy, *A Reading of Jane Austen*, London, 1975.

D. D. Devlin, *Jane Austen and Education*, London, 1975.

Ellen Moers, *Literary Women*, London, 1977.

Elaine Showalter, *A Literature of Their Own*, Princeton, 1977.

Susan Gubar, Sandra Gilbert, *The Madwoman in the Attic*, New Haven, 1979.

Warren Roberts, *Jane Austen and the French Revolution*, London, 1979.

Julia Prewitt Brown, *Jane Austen's Novels: Social Change and Literary Form*, Cambridge, Mass., 1979.

——Review Essay, *Novel*, 23 (1989), 303–13.

David Monaghan, *Jane Austen: Structure and Social Vision*, London, 1980.

D. A. Miller, *Narrative and its Discontents: Problems of Closure in the Traditional Novel*, Princeton, 1981.

Margaret Kirkham, *Jane Austen: Feminism and Fiction*, Brighton, 1983.

Mary Poovey, *The Proper Lady and the Woman Writer: Ideology as Style . . .*, Chicago, 1984.

Carole Fabricant, 'The Aesthetics and Politics of Landscape in the Eighteenth Century', in Ralph Cohen, ed., *Studies in Eighteenth-Century British Art and Aesthetics*, Los Angeles and London, 1985, 49–81.

Tony Tanner, *Jane Austen*, London, 1986.

J. F. Burrows, *Computation into Criticism: A Study of Jane Austen's Novels and an Experiment in Method*, Oxford, 1987.

Mary Evans, *Jane Austen and the State*, London and New York, 1987.

Kate Fullbrook, 'Jane Austen and the Comic Negative', in Sue Roe, ed., *Women reading Women's Writing*, Brighton, 1987.

Park Honan, *Jane Austen: Her Life*, London, 1987.

Franco Moretti, *The Way of the World: The Bildungsroman in European Culture*, London, 1987.

Claudia L. Johnson, *Jane Austen: Women, Politics and the Novel*, Chicago, 1988.

Gene Koppel, *The Religious Dimension of Jane Austen's Novels*, Ann Arbor and London, 1988.

James Thompson, *Between Self and World: the Novels of Jane Austen*, Pennsylvania, 1988.

Nancy Armstrong, *Desire and Domestic Fiction: A Political History of the Novel*, New York and Oxford, 1987.

Barbara J. Horwitz, *Jane Austen and the Question of Women's Education*, New York, 1991.

Oliver MacDonagh, *Jane Austen: Real and Imagined Worlds*, New Haven, 1991.

Meenakshi Mukherjee, *Jane Austen*, Basingstoke, 1991.

Eve Kosovsky Sedgwick, 'Jane Austen and the Masturbating Girl', *Critical Inquiry*, 17 (1990–91), 818–37.

Myra Stokes, *The Language of Jane Austen: A Study of Some Aspects of Her Vocabulary*, Basingstoke, 1991.

Rogert Gard, *Jane Austen's Novels: The Art of Clarity*, New Haven and London, 1992.

Glenda A. Hudson, *Sibling Love and Incest in Jane Austen's Fiction*, Basingstoke, 1992.

Deborah Kaplan, *Jane Austen Among Women*, Baltimore, 1992.

Gene W. Ruoff, *Jane Austen's Sense and Sensibility*, Hemel Hempstead, 1992.

John Wiltshire, *Jane Austen and the Body: 'The Picture of Health'*, Cambridge, 1992.